Let Them See You Sweat

Lessons I've Learned on My Personal Journey with Stress

Michael Levin

Published by
Hybrid Global Publishing
355 Lexington Avenue
New York, NY 10017

Copyright © 2017 by Michael Levin

All rights reserved. No part of this book may be reproduced or transmitted in any form or by in any means, electronic or mechanical, including photocopying, recording, or by any information storage and retrieval system, without the written permission of the Publisher, except where permitted by law.

Manufactured in the United States of America, or in the United Kingdom when distributed elsewhere.

Levin, Michael
Let Them See You Sweat
Lessons I've Learned on My Personal Journey with Stress
ISBN:
Paperback: 978-1-938015-54-0
eBook: 978-1-938015-55-7

Cover design by: Joe Potter
Interior design: Scribe Inc.

Author's URL: www.csiconsultinginc.com

I have had the pleasure of teaching workshops with Michael for a number of years. He has the innate ability to connect with others and share from the heart. I have seen him go through some of his journey and he has a story very much worth telling. I believe so many of us will gain tremendous value to either help ourselves or others through Michael's lessons learned due to the significant damage stress can cause.

Jeanne-Marie Grumet, CEO
Communication Catalysts, Inc.
Co-Author of *101 Great Ways to Improve Your Life*
with Jack Canfield, John Gray and Bob Proctor

The meaning of life is to find your gift.
The purpose of life is to give it away.

—Pablo Picasso

Contents

	Introduction	*vii*
1	Why I'm Telling My Story	1
2	I Thought I Was Dead	5
3	Cruising	8
4	Something Is Very Wrong, and I Don't Know What	14
5	Money Can Buy You Stress	22
6	Let Them See You Sweat	30
7	Let Them See You Sweat: Part 2	41
8	The Blood Is Flowing	54
9	The Harshest Lesson Yet	64
10	Lessons Learned	83
11	Books from Heaven?	87
12	Helping Others	90
13	My Personal Top 15 Lessons Learned	96

Introduction

When it comes to stress and its effects, I personally have been surprised by both the physical impacts and how often they go undiagnosed.

That was certainly the case for me and many others I've known. I think the lack of diagnosis can be exacerbated because the effects of stress can be delayed. I had thought of stress as a real-time occurrence. One could experience stress, and then there could be a physical reaction. What I came to realize is how strong our bodies can be in order to get us through stressful situations. And if we don't take care of our bodies after the stressful situations reduce or pass, our bodies can send us strong messages.

If we are fortunate enough to figure out that our physical issues are caused by stress, we often search for solutions in pills or bottles. My belief is that while these can provide temporary relief, unless we also look inward and learn how to take care of ourselves, the problems persist.

I have personally gotten some very strong messages. Some have been the more typical physical reactions that you might expect. I've had brain fog, chest pains, light-headedness, and dizziness. My cholesterol rose and my thyroid went out of whack. While the Western community gave me pills to fix it, they never bothered to look for the root cause of the issue. There had been a stressful period in my life that had passed. My body got me through it. But I just didn't give it a break when things got better.

One of the things that helped me was something a counselor I was seeing recommended. She wanted me to keep a journal. And I did. For several years. I found it to be cathartic and very helpful. It has also been a critical tool for me to be able to share my story with you.

I've gotten the chance to grow from these experiences. I learn and continue to learn. This is a journey. By sharing my story, I hope to give others the chance to heal, and I've been fortunate to see some miracles occur.

One such miracle is about a friend of mine, Chris. He and his wife had wanted to have children. They had been unable to and were nearing that age when they felt it would be no longer possible. They had tried all possible options to have a baby, and none had worked. Their doctor told them they would never be able to have children.

Chris and I talked about the possibility of stress impacting their ability to have children. I shared my ideas as to how it could create a block. It gave him hope, and he talked with his wife.

Today, Chris and his wife have two beautiful baby girls, Jasmine and Valeria. They were born 11 days apart. Neither one was adopted, both are their own, and they are not twins. For the rest of this story, you'll have to read my book and share my journey with me.

CHAPTER 1

Why I'm Telling My Story

This is a story I've debated about sharing. I've debated for several reasons. The first is that I knew my message wasn't "See what I've overcome." I personally feel like this is a lifetime journey, and there isn't a destination—just ongoing personal growth and learning. I am proud of what I've accomplished with regards to dealing with stress. I also know I have a ways to go, and it's a daily focus. I'm the one who created what I've needed to overcome. It took years before I realized that what was happening to me was something I had done to myself.

I've also debated telling my story because it is very personal. I've shared openly with people I'm close to in my life. Their support has made a tremendous difference in helping me on my journey. I wasn't sure if I was open to sharing the things that I went through with anyone outside my own circle.

I began to realize that sharing what I have been through with those close to me has made a difference in some of their lives. I told a little of the story about my friend Chris in the introduction. I'll share the full story and others later in the book.

I believe many people can relate to what I have gone through. Not necessarily all my symptoms, because I've experienced some that have been quite unusual. It has caused some hesitancy for me to tell my story, as some of them are a bit graphic. But I also knew I couldn't tell my story without sharing that part. I seemed to need to be hit over the head at times to get the message. And when I didn't fully get it or make the necessary changes, I kept getting hit a little harder. However, my symptoms (many of which I'll share later) have diminished. I'd like to think that although I'm still learning my lessons, I've started to get it.

I also felt that the hammers I kept getting hit with were a bit excessive. I was working on my challenges when a new hammer hit. I felt there might be a dual message. One is that I wasn't fully getting the message. The other is that I needed to tell my story. If the hammer hits weren't as hard, I might not have realized I had something to share that could help others. At the same time, maybe I just have a thick skull.

Another hesitancy I had about telling my story is that while I've definitely had some hard hits, many people have been through so much worse. That's why it's important for me to emphasize that this book is not about what I've accomplished and overcome. It's about what I've learned and can share. If it helps anyone see something in themselves or others that's helpful, then my book has served its purpose.

I know many of us can relate to dealing with stress. With what I've been through and researched, I think I've learned a lot about it. I didn't know pushing too hard and stress were what initiated many of my issues. The effects stress and panic attacks were having on my body went undiagnosed for more than a year. And it wasn't a doctor who figured it out; it was a friend.

I know I am far from alone in that many of us are suffering physical symptoms caused by stress, and we are completely unaware that it's the cause. Another factor is that I didn't understand the delayed effects of stress. I came to learn that the effects of stress don't always happen in the moment.

I think in today's times, when we are always connected, without being able to escape from our computers, phones, and other electronic devices, we don't get a chance to shut down. I'm still guilty and don't unplug often enough. I find it very easy to slip into old habits and to feel like I always have to be accessible to others.

What I am learning is how to take care of myself while not sacrificing what else is important in my life to me or others I care for. Creating more of a balance is imperative. A lot of subtle things have helped me learn that I can take care of myself without feeling selfish or being selfish. And that it can be more selfish of me not to take care of myself.

I know many friends and people I have met can relate to my story as well as the effects of stress and the damage it can do. I also am a big believer in self-healing versus finding a solution exclusively in a bottle or a pill. While I am extremely grateful for Western medicine,

I thoroughly appreciate a more holistic approach and recognize that there is no shortcut—I've got to do the hard work. If I think I'm going to solve my problems strictly with a pill, I'm just going to mask what's really going on.

Throughout the book, after all but the next chapter, I'll share the key lessons I've learned. At the end, I'll give you my top 15.

Now let me tell you my story.

CHAPTER 2

I Thought I Was Dead

It was the day that changed my life. I just didn't know it until years later.

I was at my friend Kris's house. We were having a small gathering of good friends and business partners. Kris, Paul, and I owned a business in the automotive industry. Paul ran our Colorado division, and he was in town, as we were discussing strategies. Kris's wife and two kids were there. My girlfriend at the time was there as well.

We had been drinking some wine and enjoying each other's company. Kris had a sports court in his backyard. Paul and I and Kris's kids started playing basketball. Paul is a big guy, a rugby player, and we were banging on each other pretty good. I'm not small: I'm about 6'1" and I weigh 190 pounds, and Paul still had me by a couple of inches and a good 60 pounds. After a while, I noticed I was hot and my body was tingling. I wasn't tired, just hot. I wasn't exactly dressed for basketball in jeans and a wool shirt. It was also a warm day.

I was trying to cool off but couldn't. My behavior was becoming odd, but I don't think I was fully aware of it. I was drinking water, splashing water on myself, and couldn't seem to cool down. I took off my shirt and still couldn't get cool.

My girlfriend, aside from my odd behavior, could clearly see it in my eyes. She asked if I was all right. It had been about an hour since I had stopped playing basketball. Initially, I said yes. Then I had a feeling I was in trouble. I told her no, and please call an ambulance.

Then I stopped breathing. I literally just stopped. It was the scariest feeling I've ever experienced. I wasn't hyperventilating. I just couldn't breathe. I thought I was going to die. I had no idea what would start my breathing again.

They were helping me into the front yard, and I'm pretty sure I could hear the ambulance siren. Then I passed out.

When I woke up, I was breathing again. The ambulance was pulling up. I felt OK. The paramedics checked me out while I was lying on the ground. I said I was fine. They checked my blood pressure, and it was 81 over 50. The paramedics said, "You're coming with us." I spent most of the night in the hospital rehydrating with an IV.

Later that night, I went home. I felt fine and grateful to be alive. I had suffered a bout of heatstroke and survived. This is an extremely difficult night to write about, as I can picture everything so vividly. I find myself holding my breath as I write this. There is no doubt I still have lingering effects from this memory.

Still, I thought I was fine and went back to living my life as I always had. I thought this was a one-time incident. I hadn't been very smart playing basketball with alcohol in my system, no hydration, and wearing a wool shirt and jeans on a hot day.

I had no idea at the time that it was just the beginning. And it was going to be a few years later until I found out.

CHAPTER 3

Cruising

It had been two years since my heatstroke experience. As I mentioned, I had assumed I was being foolish and just living life as I always had. I also assumed that there were no ongoing ill effects.

My tendency has always been to push. No excuses. Suck it up. I could get through anything. It was how I lived my life. If things were tough, I sucked it up and moved on.

I always put a lot of pressure on myself to be successful. I stressed about money regardless of how well I was doing. I had done very well in business overall. I've also been an entrepreneur, launching my own ventures. It's been more than 20 years since I've worked for anyone.

As most entrepreneurs experience, there are ups and downs—sometimes very significant ones. When it's your own money, your savings, your retirement at risk, it definitely changes your perspective. There is no paycheck coming in every two weeks. That was my choice and how I liked to live. I could easily have had the same stress, worrying if I was going to keep my job, if I was still working for someone else.

Because I'm an entrepreneur and frequently work out of my home office, many have asked me how I stay disciplined. However, I've found the opposite to be true for me: I couldn't turn it off. Taking a real vacation and shutting everything off was impossible for me. Who was going to take care of my customers or my clients if I didn't? How was I going to produce enough income if I wasn't working?

I've always been self-sufficient and never wanted to be a burden to anyone else. I felt like I could take care of myself. My parents died when I was young. While I wish they were still here and miss them, I also feel very fortunate that they gave me a good foundation. I've needed to rely on myself since I was 18 and didn't have parents I could lean on or call up for advice. I also felt like I had been given the tools I needed and that I'd be fine. Plus, 18 didn't seem that young to me. When others felt badly for me, I honestly felt like so many others had it worse, and I didn't deserve their sympathy.

I have always been good at taking care of others. At the same time, I found it hard to allow myself to be taken care of by someone else. What I didn't realize was that I actually wasn't taking very good care of myself.

I had no idea that what happened two years earlier was going to be the beginning of a life-changing experience. Not only was I going to need to learn how to take care of myself, but I was going to need to learn how to accept help and support from others. I was about to find out.

I was on a cruise with my buddy Todd and some other friends. We were having a great time. We had enjoyed a day of touring around Belize and zip-lining. It was around 11:00 at night and we were dancing on the ship.

Aside from one glass of wine, I hadn't been drinking. I had been drinking plenty of water. It was quite hot in the ship's club, but I didn't think anything of it. I had gone up to get drinks for a few of us and dropped them off. Then I felt the symptoms, and memories of two years earlier rushed into my head.

My arms and lips started tingling. It was all too familiar. Even though it had been two years, I knew immediately what was going on. I was having another heat incident.

I did what I typically did. I didn't want to be a burden on anyone else, including my friends. I felt I could take care of myself. I didn't even bother telling Todd. I went to our room to take a cold shower and hoped I caught it early enough. Unfortunately, that wasn't the case.

The shower wasn't working. I knew I was in trouble. Todd had no idea where I was, and I didn't have time to tell him. I contacted the infirmary and said I needed immediate help.

They gave me an IV and medication along with a shot to help me calm down. A few hours later, my body began to recover. The nurse was able to locate Todd and let him know what was going on. Needless to say, he was angry. He had no idea where I was. I was operating under my usual philosophy of not wanting to be a burden. I knew Todd would be there for me, as would the majority of my friends. This was all about me not being willing to ask for help and support when I needed it.

This was the beginning of one of many lessons I was about to receive. I needed to learn to not always suck it up and try to push through. It was the beginning of learning how to accept and ask for support from those in my life.

You would think this would be enough for me to get it, to be willing to ask others for help. Allow those close to me to provide support when I needed it. Especially because my friends were not only willing to provide support; they wanted to. I definitely hadn't learned my lesson yet from this experience. But I started to get it. I had, and still have, a ways to go.

The next day, a group was going to a park in Playa del Carmen. I badly wanted to go. Even though Todd and other friends wanted me to take it easy and relax on the ship, I refused. I felt, just like always, I could suck it up and push through.

I walked to the ferry that would take us to the park and realized I had absolutely no chance of going. My body wasn't even remotely right. I was angry that I was missing out on this opportunity and angry with myself that I couldn't push through.

I also didn't realize that this was to become the beginning of having to learn I couldn't always push through. I couldn't always suck it up. It was no longer going to be an option. If I wasn't going to make the conscious choice to be better to myself, my body was going to make it for me.

My Lessons Learned

From this day forward, I knew that I would never do again what I did with Todd. While to this day, it's still not easy for me to ask for help, I know that those in my life will help me if I ask. Even more so, they want to help. I'm minimizing our friendship by not trusting them enough to be open with them and share that I need help when I'm in a situation like this.

I'm also learning more to take care of myself, which also includes asking those around me for support. I fly quite a bit, and if I have a window seat, I hate to bug the people next to me if I need to use the restroom. I know I'm far from alone in regard to feeling this way. In order to take care of myself, I now do one of two things. First, if I am in the window seat, I'll ask. Second, if it's a long flight, I try to book or sit in an aisle seat. I don't mind letting other people out at all. It goes back to the trait I mentioned earlier: I feel like I'm good at taking care of others. This can go for not only those I'm close to but strangers as well. By taking the aisle seat, I accomplish both. I can take care of myself and others.

To me, taking care of yourself and respecting that your friends (or possibly strangers) want to help can be powerful. I've tried to learn new habits, even simple ones, to not minimize myself or someone who might want to help me. When I'm traveling, there are times when I dine out alone. I used to do what I think many others do when that occurs. I would say, "Just one, please." We minimize ourselves, and we're a burden because we'd like a table and we're dining alone. Plus, we're going to be a small bill for the waitstaff.

I've changed what I say in order to help reflect my new attitude. I take out the word "just." I now say, "One, please." I take care of myself and don't minimize myself even if I'm eating alone. I also tip well when the service is good because the waitstaff has taken care of me, and I do know I'm a smaller tip than a table of four, yet they are probably checking on me almost as often. I want to thank them for not minimizing me either.

I'll share more on this topic later, as this only scratches the surface of learning how to take care of myself and allowing those in my life to support me.

CHAPTER 4

Something Is Very Wrong, and I Don't Know What

I was in Southern California at my friend Mark's house for the weekend. Leading up to that weekend, over the prior month, I had felt off. There was a tingling feeling throughout my body. Not that I would know personally, but from how others I knew had described it, I got the sense it might be as if I had early multiple sclerosis symptoms. I didn't think that's what it was, but I also felt that it was quite serious and potentially life threatening.

I had no idea what to do about it. I didn't even know whom I should see. I had gone to my chiropractor for an adjustment to see if that would help, but it didn't.

I continued to feel off throughout the weekend with Mark. Not long before I was going to fly home, he and I went into their backyard to play Wiffle ball with his son and his friend. We played for about a half hour. It was pretty warm out. It had been about two years since my heatstroke bout on the cruise ship, but I also had a couple of near misses. My body had clearly become much more sensitive to heat. It didn't take nearly as much for me to become affected.

I had been drinking a tremendous amount of water. When we were done playing, I packed and took a shower, and we were off to the airport. Over an hour had passed since we played. I still felt a bit off, and Mark was blasting his air conditioning for me. As we were nearing the airport, the symptoms came on. I knew I was experiencing another bout of heatstroke. I told Mark he needed to find a hospital quick.

Nothing was close. We had a lengthy drive back to a hospital near his house. Learning from my episode with Todd, I told Mark I needed him to be my advocate. I was no longer going to prevent my friends from supporting me. When we got to the hospital, they quickly got an IV in me. This time, though, the IV didn't make me feel better. I started to experience serious chest pains. I thought I might be having a heart attack. Mark was there, making sure I was being taken care of and staying on top of the medical staff to find the cause of the problem.

They eventually found what they believed was the source of my chest pains: my system was badly depleted of potassium. The doctor found I drank so much water I had flushed the potassium out of my system, and he felt that was what caused the chest pains. After I took a potassium tablet, I began to feel better.

I was warned I was going to feel off for at least a week because of the potassium depletion along with the heatstroke. I felt good that night and decided to fly out the next morning, against Mark's wishes. He wanted me to stay for a few days. I wanted to get back to work. As usual, I was pushing. What I didn't know at the time was that I wasn't going to feel OK in a week or two. I wasn't going to be even close to right for a very long time.

The feeling I had the prior month started to get worse. I felt light-headed. I was experiencing chest pains on a frequent basis. It felt like I was at risk of a heart attack, as the pains were both random and at times sharp.

I couldn't get my brain to work properly. I couldn't put my thoughts together. Things that would normally be easy to remember, I couldn't. I would see someone I had known for years and couldn't remember his or her name. It was obvious to my friends. They could tell I couldn't grasp things I would normally recall easily. My brain felt like it was constantly in a fog.

I was also regularly and randomly experiencing shortness of breath. I would be driving and all of a sudden couldn't breathe. I'd roll down the windows and bring as much air in as I could, waiting and hoping for it to pass.

I started seeing different specialists. I saw an endocrinologist, who found my thyroid was off. It had always been normal, but it no longer was. I wanted to give it a little time and see if my thyroid would return to normal, as I hate taking medication. After a few months with no improvement, I was told I had no choice but to go on thyroid meds.

I still wasn't feeling any better on thyroid meds. It made literally no difference for me except my thyroid numbers were normal. I talked to the endocrinologist to see what else she could recommend. She said that if my thyroid numbers were normal, she had done all she could. Clearly, I was hoping for a little more.

My cholesterol had always been normal. Now my cholesterol was off as well. I didn't want to take cholesterol meds. All the specialists I saw, though, felt I absolutely needed to. They felt I was putting myself at risk with my numbers. My diet hadn't changed. My exercise hadn't changed. Yet my cholesterol had changed—dramatically. I agreed to go on cholesterol meds.

Just to add one more thing to the list, I developed food allergies. This was the least of my worries, yet it was still an additional problem. I never had any food allergies previously. Then I ate a shrimp dish I had numerous times before and had an anaphylactic reaction. I had hundreds of hives all over my body, and my face swelled up like a balloon. I also shortly thereafter developed allergies to crab, lobster, and wheat.

I saw a neurologist to have my brain scanned. I had lost a very good friend to a brain tumor. I wanted to find out if I was suffering from the same. The neurologist didn't think that's what it was but thought we should check. The tests showed up clear. He had no other tests or ideas with respect to the cause of my brain fog and light-headedness.

I saw a cardiologist as well who was clearly a proponent for cholesterol meds. Still, I was suffering from chest pains regularly, as well as shortness of breath. He had me wear a heart monitor for a month. Every time I felt a pain, I pressed a button that caused a report to be generated by a monitoring company.

At the end of the month, we met. He said I had an arrhythmia, and though it might cause an occasional pain, I wasn't at risk. He said he had one as well. He didn't have an explanation for why I felt pain, aside from the occasional arrhythmic reaction.

I had run out of specialists. Between all my doctors—my GP, the endocrinologist, the neurologist, and the cardiologist—I had no answers. And I was getting worse.

I could no longer exercise like I used to. A short bike ride would exacerbate my light-headedness and dizziness. I'd feel exhausted. I would feel claustrophobic, as though the walls were closing in on me. I forgot what normal felt like because I literally never felt normal.

That became more obvious when, for some reason, one day I had this brief moment—roughly 15 minutes—where I experienced absolute clarity. Everything was normal. It was how I used to always feel. The fog went away. After 15 minutes, the fog and the rest of my symptoms came back. I was no longer clear. I continued to feel that whatever I had was potentially life threatening, and I had no idea what it was or what to do.

Then one day a friend of mine, a former nurse, asked me to come into her home office. She had been doing some research. She had a page up on her computer titled "Panic Attacks." They could have had my picture next to the symptoms. I had all of them. Finally, I could put a name to what I was experiencing.

For some reason, none of the doctors thought of it. They were so locked into traditional Western medicine issues that they never considered the possibility that a significant portion of my problems were emotional, not medical.

My GP tested our theory by putting me on an anti-anxiety medication. The fog started to clear. While I wasn't fully back to normal, I was dramatically better. I now knew my problem. I also knew I had to do something about it aside from taking pills. I knew they were addictive. I knew this was something I needed to work on myself, and I needed to start on my journey to help myself heal naturally.

My Lessons Learned

This was quite a lesson for me. While I've always had a holistic side to me, I had relied on Western medicine to diagnose my issues. Years ago, I got licensed as a massage therapist. One of the things I remember learning in the classes that stood out to me was when the instructor said that each person's body, when given the opportunity, will try to seek its own state of rightness.

What he meant by that is if you give your body a chance to be healthy and to function as it should, it will do its best to operate that way. For example, when it comes to massage, I've found I can put someone's neck back in if his or her vertebrae are out. I don't do it through an adjustment. That's not something I'd try, nor do I know how to do it. I help create space where the vertebrae are supposed to be, and most times they will slide back in where they belong. I give the body a chance to find its state of rightness, and the body does the rest.

Yet somehow, even though I fully believe in doing things more naturally, I never considered that the problem wasn't physical and that emotional causes could be creating physical symptoms. I don't like taking pills, not even aspirin. Yet I only sought out doctors who focused on physical symptoms.

I've also found others in my life who have experienced the same. If you go to doctors who focus on Western issues, they will also focus on Western solutions. Because their exploration was only for physical causes, they didn't explore mental and emotional issues that could be causing my problems. I believe this is something many can probably relate to. When I tell my story, I can't tell you how often people will tell me they either have personally had similar experiences or know of others who have.

Later, I'll tell you about others who have had physical issues that turned out to be stress. My friend Mark, whom I told you about in this chapter, years later developed significant enough chest pains that his doctors recommended an angiogram and a full work-up. When nothing was found, they never even considered the possibility that stress might be causing his problems. Mark didn't consider it until he and I spoke after his tests. More on Mark's story later.

I also think we tend to ignore stress because it can seem weak to acknowledge that we're having problems with it. A physical issue can be a dinnertime topic or a badge of courage. But acknowledging that you're having mental or physical problems due to stress can sound like you don't know how to manage it or you aren't strong or tough enough to deal with it. I know I've offered my help to some who haven't taken me up on it. I believe a big reason is that it feels embarrassing to them. It can make them feel weak.

I also believe stress has become such a pervasive part of our society that we get used to it and frequently don't recognize its effects. I certainly didn't. I'm not saying I wouldn't explore the Western side for symptoms. At the same time, to ignore or not consider what symptoms stress might be causing could lead you to constantly trying to find a solution in a pill or a bottle. And in reality, the greatest solution can come from within, by making lifestyle changes and knowing that if you give your body the chance, it will do its best to seek its own state of rightness.

CHAPTER 5

Money Can Buy You Stress

The cause of the panic attacks and the stress didn't make sense to me. Things were going well in my life. My consulting practice was taking off. My personal life was good. Although I was pushing hard like I always did, I wasn't feeling unusually stressed.

I know that I can stress over two things in particular: time and money. I can put a lot of pressure on myself to always rush and never be late for anything or anybody, and I feel like I can't possibly complete everything I need to get done.

Then I began to realize and uncover what happened. While things were good now, about six months before I felt the symptoms, I had been going through a tough period that had lasted for about two years.

During this two-year stretch, I experienced financial struggles. I have been an entrepreneur for more than 20 years and haven't had a regular paycheck from a job during that time. I had been fortunate and always done very well. This was my first bout of struggling. I didn't handle it well.

I had a successful business I had sold. I was trying to start a consulting practice and real estate investment business. Neither was doing well. The economy was terrible, and I was paying the price. It was something I had never experienced. Either whatever I had started in the past worked or I had enough positive ventures going that those that didn't make it didn't take me down.

I didn't know how to handle it. Then, to make matters worse, I had a friend who was a financial planner managing my money. Through some bad maneuvers, he literally lost everything I had in the stock market in a matter of hours. I had a couple of real estate investments in projects that went bankrupt. My level of stress was off the charts.

Now things were good, though. I didn't experience panic attacks before, when I easily could have and should have the way I was driving myself and stressing about my situation. I couldn't figure out why it was happening now. I didn't feel stressed. But my body clearly did.

I began to understand the possible delayed reaction of stress. I had thought stress occurred in real time, but I was learning that wasn't necessarily the case. I now know others who have experienced the same.

I met with holistic practitioners as well to gain a better understanding as to what was going on with my body. I found out my adrenals were shot. During my time of stress, apparently my body produced enough adrenaline and cortisol to carry me through. I had worn my body out during that time, and I didn't slow down when things got better. Now I was paying the price.

It was difficult for me to figure out what to do, because aside from how I stress about not having enough time, I didn't feel like I was experiencing much stress in my life. But I had this condition that was absolutely debilitating at times.

I was driving one day and was coming up to a red light. My mind and body didn't recognize it, though. I wasn't functioning right. Just as I was coming to the intersection, I noticed it. I slammed on my brakes, but there was no chance of stopping in time. There was oncoming traffic.

My reactions came back just in time for me to turn my wheel sharply and put my car into a sideways skid. Just before I was going to hit another car, I floored it, got my car going forward, and was able to miss them. It made me realize that driving wasn't safe until I could get this fixed. But I still had to drive. I had to find a way to work through it.

I came to realize I needed to make lifestyle changes. Because I ate pretty well and exercised, I thought I was taking care of my body. I began to understand I needed to do more than that. I was still pushing myself too hard, trying to be everything I could for my clients and to make sure I was successful. I was also involved in a new business, and I felt like I couldn't support my staff.

A new stress had been added because I was nervous I couldn't perform well for my clients due to my lack of mental clarity. Most people in my life, except for those

I was closest to, didn't know about my issues. On the outside, I seemed calm.

I decided to take a bold step and acknowledge I had a problem. I needed to share what I was going through with others. I decided to tell my clients. I was concerned my clients might decide they didn't want to work with me anymore. It was a chance I felt I needed to take.

I also felt I should disclose to my staff what was going on. My feeling was that I should be their support, not the other way around. I wanted them to know they could count on me. But could they feel I'd be able to lead them if I seemed "weak"? I'll tell you more about those conversations later in this book.

I was taking more time for myself, trying to learn how to relax, practicing deep breathing. I was reading about how to take care of myself naturally and had started doing some acupuncture as well.

It felt good to at least know what was going on and that I could begin to put a plan together to help heal myself. I was stunned that stress could cause such damage. From what I learned, it seemed that my adrenals and immune system were compromised by what I had put my body and mind through. I felt my cholesterol and thyroid issues, along with the allergies, were all tied to the stress I created in my body.

My panic attacks and light-headedness certainly weren't going away completely. But they were improving. There were more and more moments of clarity. One day I just decided to quit the antianxiety meds cold turkey. I know you're supposed to wean off them, but I decided I'd had enough and was going to do this on my own. As I said, I was never big on taking pills. As much as I wanted the ease of solving my issues with a pill, I felt to solve my problem required effort and change on my part. I didn't feel I could get where I needed to be if I was going to be reliant on a pill. Plus, I didn't want to be addicted to anything.

What I didn't know at that time, despite the headway I was making, was that my journey was only beginning, and it was going to get harder. Although I was making changes, they weren't sufficient. The messages I had received from my body to date were fairly commonplace. I was about to get some unusual and harsh ones to let me know I still had a lot of work to do.

My Lessons Learned

As you are probably gathering, while I was definitely learning, this was going to be a lengthy journey. As I share my lessons, I'm trying to be accurate as to what I had learned up to each of these moments without jumping ahead.

And that is part of my lesson. This is a journey—something I have to work on and improve every day.

My biggest lesson here was the delayed effects of stress. It never hit me, or any of the Western doctors, that stress could be a cause. While my doctors didn't explore it, the way my life was going certainly wouldn't have been a giveaway. They needed to explore my past to find out.

Michael Levin

As I mentioned, I was doing fine. I didn't realize that by continuing to push and not altering my lifestyle when things were better, my body would say, "Enough is enough. If you aren't going to take care of yourself, I'm going to make you. I hung in there for you during the tough times. Now I need a break, and if you aren't going to give me one, I'm going to take one."

I believe it's common for us to push ourselves without recognizing the damage it does. That was certainly the case for me. This doesn't mean we can't work hard, be motivated, and strive to be successful. It just means there has to be a balance. We have to take care of ourselves too. And it doesn't take that much time. We clean our cars and homes and make sure they're in good repair. Frequently, though, I believe we may not do the same for ourselves. While I felt I was doing so by eating pretty decently and going to the gym, it wasn't enough.

I know I continue to push, as I never want to make excuses or seem weak whether at work or play. I feel like I should suck it up. Because of that philosophy, I had another near heatstroke bout at my niece's Bat Mitzvah party. We were playing dodgeball, volleyball, and air hockey, among other activities.

A few days before the event, a good buddy of mine reminded me not to push it. He said I always do and get myself in trouble. Sure enough, we were playing and I was having a great time. It was in an indoor play space, and it was warm. I stopped in the middle of a volleyball game, as I started to feel off. I wasn't tired at all. I just felt hot and like I should stop.

It turns out I was on the edge of overheating and almost needed to be hospitalized. My brother-in-law came over to check on me, and I told him what was going on. I was pissed off, as everyone else was still playing, and I said, "I don't get it. I'm in better shape than most of them, yet they aren't having any problems." He corrected me and said, "You're more fit than most of them."

After a time, I got the distinction he was trying to make. I worked out, I wasn't overweight, and some of them didn't exercise at all. Yet I was the one in trouble. I was more fit, but I wasn't in better shape. I didn't take care of myself inside and out the way I needed to. So while some of them may have been overweight or out of shape by traditional measures, they were actually *in better shape* than me because they took care of themselves in ways that I didn't.

I was vulnerable to heat and still didn't want to fully admit it. I was still trying to make my body push through versus understanding what my new reality was and taking care of myself.

This same buddy who told me to take it easy at the Bat Mitzvah party also had given me a great piece of advice that I chose to ignore. When I sold one of my businesses, he suggested that I take some time off and enjoy myself. Stop and smell the roses for a while. I ignored it for two reasons. First, I didn't want to live off my savings. I felt fortunate that we had built a successful business and sold it. At the same time, I felt like I needed to replace the income that business provided. Instead, I put a tremendous amount of pressure on myself and stressed. It was the first time I didn't have a steady income of some kind in 16 years. I should have taken his advice, as it would have been very healthy for me.

Financial issues were a real trigger for me. Shortly after I got out of college, I had rented an apartment with a friend. At the last minute, my friend bailed on me. I decided to keep the apartment. I had just gotten my first job, but it didn't work out. All of a sudden, I had no job, almost no savings, an apartment payment, and a car payment. Going out for a sandwich was a real treat.

I felt like it was my responsibility to get this turned around. I'd never ask for help. This was despite the fact that I had some insurance money from my father's death, and my uncle managed the account. He would have helped me if I had asked. But I didn't even consider it. It never entered my mind to ask him. I felt like I got myself into this situation, and it was up to me to get myself out of it.

I had this heightened level of responsibility, and it was difficult for me to ask others for help. There was a time about two years later when I was in a similar financial position after I lost a job and needed a little help. That time, I decided to talk to my uncle and not completely stress myself out. He was happy to help, and I only needed that assistance for two weeks. Somehow, this was a lesson I forgot later in life. Those in my life were happy to help and support me, and knew I'd never take advantage of them.

CHAPTER 6

Let Them See You Sweat

With the combination of my heat issues and panic attacks, my first harsh message came. My body stopped sweating. I believe, without a doubt, that my last heatstroke and my body stopping sweating were, at the least, caused partially by stress.

Since my third heatstroke incident, my tolerance to heat had dramatically reduced. I could get light-headed and dizzy on an 80-degree day with no humidity if I was out in the sun. It could sometimes happen when it was even cooler if I was in direct sun. I could also have a hard time if I was inside and it was stuffy and hot.

Not being able to sweat was making things much more challenging. My body couldn't cool off. When I was in any situation that was warm, it felt like the inside of my body was a microwave.

I was still working out but had to be very careful and pace myself. I'd take walks early in the morning or later at night. In the gym, I cut back significantly on my formerly intense workouts, drank a lot of water, and paced myself.

I was fighting several emotional issues around this too. First, I had always been very active. I didn't let much hold me back. I was injury prone playing sports and have torn just about everything at least once. Still, I'd be back playing as soon as possible, frequently playing through my injuries. I played outfield in softball and one year tore a tendon in my arm and literally couldn't throw a ball two feet. For some reason, though, it didn't bother me when I hit.

I played the outfield the entire season without being able to throw. One of the other outfielders would come over and get the ball from me to throw it in. I guess I did enough other things well, so they accommodated me. I knew that if I could, I would suck it up and play.

I also wanted someone in my life, and although I have lived with two women long term, I have never been married. I wanted to be. I typically dated women who were active as well. With my heat issues, I felt like I would hold back anyone I was dating. I couldn't do outside activities on warmer days. With any activity, I had to be very careful. I felt badly that someone would have to accommodate me, and at times I felt weak. I felt like damaged goods. Who would want to be with me if I couldn't keep up and was holding her back?

As I mentioned earlier, my friends were great. I am very fortunate. I think most of my friends have some similar qualities. For the most part, we're all sports guys, both participants and fans. We're all pretty driven and have either our own companies or good careers. And we're also a pretty compassionate group. If we are doing an activity, whether it's golfing or a ball game, they make sure they can accommodate me so I don't get too warm. They are constantly checking with me to make sure I'm OK and keeping me in the shade as much as possible.

I needed to learn through all this that I couldn't just "suck it up." Not that I still don't, in some part, believe in that philosophy. I'm not big on excuses. I had to take care of myself. As I mentioned earlier, I always felt I was good at taking care of others in my life—just not so good at taking care of me. I thought that eating decently and exercising were enough.

This was one thing I couldn't just push through. Not that I didn't try. Aside from my three hospitalizations for heat issues, I had several other close calls. There seemed to be a cumulative effect, and I knew I couldn't keep putting my body through it.

Also, there were times when I would just get scared. I was having flashbacks to the day when I stopped breathing, passed out, and thought I was dead. When I was outside and started feeling light-headed or began to tingle, I wasn't sure what was real and what was in my head. Plus, it certainly wasn't helping my panic attack issues.

A key fear I had was that I never knew if I pushed myself too far. The effect was delayed. The first time, it was almost an hour between the time I stopped playing basketball and the time I stopped breathing and passed out. The last time, at my friend Mark's house, more than an hour had passed between the time we stopped playing and the time the symptoms came on. If I felt any symptoms, I'd be scared I had gone too far and there was no recovering from it. It was the oddest feeling to continue to feel worse and worse even though I had removed myself from the sun or heat and was trying to cool down.

Not sweating was certainly making my heat issue much more difficult and frightening. I had assumed this was a by-product of my prior heat bouts and possibly even my panic attacks. At this stage, while my panic attacks were getting better, it was still difficult to ascertain what was causing what.

Then a friend of mine had an idea. What if I started sweating again? Would that help relieve all or some of my heat issues? She had been doing some research and found a condition called anhidrosis (again, I was stunned a friend figured this out and none of the doctors had). Anhidrosis is a condition in which you have the inability to sweat normally. It certainly seemed that I had this condition. It made sense to me that if I could get my body's natural cooling mechanism working, it had to help me, at least somewhat.

I started seeing some well-regarded doctors in the Bay Area. Their solution was the same: stay out of the sun and drink lots of water. I had kind of figured that out on my own. My friend got me a referral to a neurologist at Mayo Clinic. I was excited. If there was any place that could help me, I felt it would be there. I was and still am open to exploring all Western, Eastern, and holistic solutions. I was absolutely fine with a combination of both. I knew that, regardless, there needed to be effort on my part if I was going to get well.

I flew to the Mayo Clinic in Scottsdale, Arizona, to meet with the neurologist. I told him my self-diagnosis.

He made it clear he was the doctor and he'd tell me what my situation was. At the same time, I liked him. It was apparent up front that he was different.

He reviewed my prior blood tests and was excited. He acknowledged I had the markers for anhidrosis. It was something he was quite interested in, as he had written a paper on the subject. He felt he had a couple of potential solutions to help me. He wanted to put me through a battery of tests to confirm his initial diagnosis.

The tests they had at Mayo Clinic were impressive. If you've never been, it's a completely different experience from most medical facilities. The clinic in Scottsdale felt like a resort. The facilities were beautiful. You are treated like you're a special guest. They have a great cafeteria with healthy food. They even have piano players to entertain you. It was the first time I found it somewhat enjoyable to hang around a medical facility. The only thing that seemed a bit odd was that a guy with heat issues was in Scottsdale, Arizona, where it was over 100 degrees, to try to solve his problem.

The tests they put me through were extremely sophisticated. I went home after my tests and was due to come back in a couple of weeks after my doctor could analyze the results.

The day before I was supposed to come back, I received a surprising message. I was about to leave for a client appointment. My car had been outside because I had contractors working in my house and garage. I reached into my car to get some things out, and it was very warm in the car. My body immediately started sweating—enough that I actually had to go back in and change my shirt. It had been such a long time since my body had actually sweated, and here I was sweating profusely.

All I could do was smile. I knew then when I went to the Mayo Clinic the next day, the markers my doctor saw on the blood tests wouldn't be present. Their sophisticated tests were going to show I didn't have anhidrosis, or at least no longer had anhidrosis. I had no delusions though about what I was experiencing. In no way did I think I was cured. In fact, the day after I got back from my follow-up Mayo Clinic trip was one of my most difficult days in terms of dealing with heat: I was feeling very light-headed and dizzy from a gym workout. And my body certainly didn't sweat profusely, if at all.

I knew I was getting a clear message: I wasn't getting my answer from a pill. I already knew that the doctor's solutions involved steroids and pills. He had shared with me that he'd had some success with these two options.

I had been doing a lot of personal growth along with Eastern and holistic medicine work to try to get better. I had been going to an acupuncturist regularly. I had been taking Chinese herbs. I had started doing Qi Gong to help with both stress and healing. I was going through counseling.

For those of you not familiar with Qi Gong, it's a Chinese practice intended to provide both meditational and medicinal benefits through movement and breathing. Whether it has helped me or not, I don't know. I do feel that anything I could do to better take care of myself, consciously dedicating time to my well-being, was beneficial.

I flew down the next day to Scottsdale. When my doctor walked into the room, he almost seemed depressed. What I expected was true. My markers were gone for anhidrosis. He said he couldn't help me. I could try the pill, one of his possible solutions, if I'd like to see if it helped.

I shared with him what I had been doing. I expected him to blow it off. Instead, he acknowledged the possible benefit of what I was doing. My feeling was to continue down this holistic path and see how it went. I told him I'd appreciate the prescription so I could have the option of trying out his pill. I wanted to start, though, by continuing to do what I had been doing. To my surprise, he agreed.

It has been several years since I went to Mayo Clinic. I am still doing a variety of holistic activities to work on my sweating. Ever since that day, my body has continued to sweat, although not remotely as profusely as it did that one day when I reached into my car.

I have to be careful to monitor myself. When I'm working out, I check how much I'm sweating. I always drink plenty of water. I sometimes use cooling towels to help. I try to get on aerobic equipment like elliptical machines that are near a fan. When I work out, I try to visualize myself sweating, breathing deeply and slowly instead of panicking and worrying if I'm pushing myself too hard. At the same time, I try to be very conscious and respectful of what's going on in my body and don't hesitate to stop if I feel I need to.

At some point during the time of dealing with stress, I decided to see a therapist as well. I thought it was important to take a comprehensive approach to working on and dealing with my stress.

I learned a lot of eye-opening things. I've referred to the fact that I had always followed the motto of "Suck it up." I've also mentioned that I lost my parents at a young age. I never felt that should be an excuse for any challenges I experienced. I felt I was very lucky that my parents had given me a solid foundation for life.

My Lessons Learned

I find it absolutely amazing that my body could sweat as profusely as it did that one day and so instantaneously. I am personally more spiritual than religious. I don't know if I was getting a message from my body or from outside of my body. I certainly acknowledge the possibility of both. The one thing I can't deny is what happened and how clear that message was. This is my journey. It is up to me to take ownership and be responsible for it. I need to take care of myself, and it certainly doesn't need to be at the expense of others. My solution wasn't coming from a pill; it was coming from within. This is a lifetime journey, and it is a journey I need to be conscious of every day. There is no destination. And isn't it the journey we're all living for anyway?

I fully admit that a frustration for me is commercials about how you can lose weight—or solve any other problem—just by taking a pill or another simple solution. I understand it's highly desirable to find an easy solution. And you can possibly help stress through antianxiety meds or antidepressants. My antianxiety meds helped me get on track. But I use don't want pills to be my only solution, and I was very glad when I was able to get off it. To use a pill as a support is one thing. But if your only solution to lose weight or to reduce stress is to pop a pill, I don't feel you are doing what you need to do to fully take care of yourself.

Another key lesson for me is that I could have attributed all my heat issues to a medical problem. It certainly started as a medical problem. I earned my first heatstroke bout by not hydrating, drinking alcohol, and playing basketball on a hot day in warm clothing. I have come to understand that once you have one bout, you are susceptible to others.

This is a permanent issue for me. I'm not trying to sound defeatist; I just believe it's realistic at this stage. While I'm not giving up, I also realize that I might never be able to be back out in the sun as I once could. I have to be very careful. I also want to continue doing whatever I can to become as heat tolerant as possible.

I do believe that part of this is medical. But at the same time, I believe the reason my body stopping sweating was part of my reaction to stress, my depleted immune system, and the inflammation and heat in my body (which I'll talk more about later). I believe that became apparent when my markers for anhidrosis disappeared and I sweated profusely that one day.

I now sweat. Not normally. Not as much as I once did. But I do sweat. Some days more than others. I can get through a gym workout most days without getting light-headed, and I rarely need a cooling towel. It's all been done through what I mentioned earlier in this chapter: reducing my stress and using therapy, acupuncture, herbs, and Qi Gong. I try to relax and not panic about it, knowing I'm OK.

I can still picture that day so vividly when my body started sweating when I reached into my car. It was a lesson to me beyond sweating. It was about looking within for answers. I still don't know exactly what works and what doesn't and what causes what reaction to help me reduce stress and tolerate heat. I know there are both physical and emotional effects. I also adjust based on how I'm doing. I've been off the herbs for a while, but I'm seeing some indicators that I'll talk about in my next chapter that tell me I need to restart. I am constantly learning, growing, and adjusting to take care of myself.

Possibly the most important lesson I've learned from not sweating is that I can't always just suck it up. I can't always push through. It's not physically possible now. It could kill me. If I wasn't going to learn on my own that I can't always push through, my body was going to provide me with a daily reminder that it isn't a possibility.

I've also learned to be more reliant on others and let myself be taken care of. My friends and family are happy to accommodate me. And it makes me feel good to allow myself to be taken care of. While I sometimes still can feel like a burden, there are many more days where it is a reminder of how lucky and grateful I am for the support I have in my life.

CHAPTER 7

Let Them See You Sweat

Part 2

This chapter ties back to the more figurative part of the title of my book. It's not about taking on the pressure, feeling it, and letting others see how stressed out you are. It's not about embracing stress and having your audience see you perspire. It's about asking for the support you need and feeling confident that your family, friends, and even business associates will stand by your side and support you.

I hadn't cut back my efforts or energy with respect either to my own businesses or to the work I was doing with my clients. Despite the fact that I was feeling awful—between the chest pains, brain fog, shortness of breath, and other symptoms—I had been able to hide it. For much of this time, my symptoms had still gone undiagnosed.

After I knew that it was stress and panic attacks, I began working on it on my own. In the initial stages, my solution was a balance of medication and lifestyle changes. Over time, I decided to get off the medication. I was definitely getting better, and I also had a way to go.

I made the decision that I needed to share what was going on with others in my life. I started with my friends. It was difficult for me, as I didn't like expressing or sharing what I felt was weakness. As I talked about earlier, a lot of my friends are sports guys and successful, and we can definitely give each other a hard time. For lack of a better term, they could be considered "guy's guys." At the same time, they all had good hearts, and I felt I could talk with them. I also have a number of female friends, and we are very open with each other.

I told them what was going on. Those whom I was closest to knew about the tests I had been going through. They also could see the difference in me that others I saw less frequently could not. They noticed I'd had difficulty remembering things. I'd find myself searching for words. I could be spacy or forgetful. I don't have the best memory, but I was even more forgetful than usual.

It was a vulnerable place to be, but I felt like I needed to be open. If it was physical, sharing would have been easy. Telling them that I'm overly stressed, not dealing with it well, and having panic attacks regularly wasn't easy. Telling them that I had literally had 10 minutes of mental clarity in the past year was difficult.

Across the board, the level of support I received was incredible. I was also surprised how many could relate.

It didn't surprise me that they were experiencing stress; what surprised me was the number that indicated they had experienced physical reactions to stress.

They wanted to know what they could do to help, what support I needed. There wasn't a single instance in which someone either took it as a weakness on my part, teased me about it, or wasn't either sympathetic or empathetic.

Being able to be honest with them was both healing and cathartic. Not having to hide things helped me relax. In the past, when I was feeling off, I would work hard not to show it. Now that wasn't necessary.

The harder steps, though, were to come. I decided to tell both my employees and my clients. There were times that I felt I couldn't support them in the way I wanted to. I was afraid I would fail them. I had done my best to hide it, and neither group was aware of my issues. Especially with regards to my staff and my clients, I didn't want to show what I felt was weakness. I felt they needed to be able to lean on me, and it was my responsibility to support them.

I felt that the fear of failing them and the undue stress I was putting on myself to push through my issues could lead to failures for them and exacerbate my problems. It took a little time for me to come to grips with the thought of disclosing my illness to them. I also felt that these conversations could go two completely different ways.

My staff probably wasn't going to say everything that was on their minds. I felt they'd be polite and were more likely to be supportive. With my clients, as they were my customers, I was concerned they might let me go and try to find someone who was more "stable" and could support them, at least at that moment.

I started with my staff. They were great. They said they hadn't realized what was going on. In meetings when I personally felt completely lost, I had somehow covered it up well enough that they hadn't noticed it, or at least they said they hadn't noticed.

They asked what they could do to help. Were there things they could take off my plate? What could they do to make things easier on me?

I didn't have to put on a façade as their leader who wasn't supposed to show weakness or fallibilities or insecurities. I found I didn't need a lot of support. Just knowing they understood, knowing I didn't have to fake it, took a lot of pressure off of me. I did delegate more, and I also gave myself slack if I didn't get everything done that I felt I needed to. There would be another day.

Telling my clients was a different story. I was extremely nervous as I set up times for each of us to talk. I wanted to meet face-to-face, as I felt it was important. Also, if disclosing this information shook their confidence in me, if they felt I wasn't the right choice, I wanted to give them the opportunity in person to decide to move on and let them know I'd respect their choice.

Every one of my clients reacted the same way. The first reaction was surprise. To them, I always seemed so calm on the outside. They would never have guessed that I'd be someone who was dealing with stress and panic attacks.

It was the persona I gave off. While I can be very open with those close to me, I know I can keep emotions in and just deal with them myself. I don't have much of a temper, and typically I really have to be pushed to become outwardly angry. I also know I internalize more than I should.

For my clients in particular, I felt they needed to see me as calm and grounded so they could feel confident that I was training and guiding them properly. I wanted them to feel like I was their security blanket and support, and I shouldn't be leaning on them for support in any way. It seemed I had been successful on that front.

The second reaction was that they were glad I told them. All asked what they could do to support me. They were grateful for all I had done for them, and all wanted to continue our relationship. There weren't any who waivered about wanting to work together. They only wanted to do what they could to help me.

I was touched and extremely grateful. I was also surprised at their reaction and that it didn't affect their confidence in me to honor my commitment to them.

I took one of them up on her offer of support. One of my reactions to the stress is that I had become shakier as a driver. Typically, if my client and I were going somewhere together, I'd drive. We were going to a trade show, and I asked if she minded driving. She said, "No problem."

I quickly realized she might have been the worst driver I had ever been with. We'd be driving on the freeway with limited traffic, and she'd just slam on her brakes for no apparent reason. She had dramatic reactions when there seemed to be no need. It was funny in a way to see this, as she was one of the kindest, nicest people I knew and always seemed very outwardly calm to me.

About halfway there, I said, "I think your driving is causing me more stress than my own driving, and I think I may be our safer option. Do you mind if we switch?" She laughed and was very kind about it, and we traded seats. She let me drive her car the rest of the way. She acknowledged driving wasn't one of her strong suits. Still, though, the level of support she provided, and the fact that we could talk so honestly, was a great lesson for me in being able to take care of myself.

I had one more step, though, in letting my friends, family, staff, and clients see me sweat. I had started losing my hair in my early 20s. It was something that had always bothered me. I had complexion challenges with pimples up until about the time I was 20. I joked that I was hoping for a few more years of enjoying the time between puberty and baldness.

About the time I was 30, I started seeing ads for hair that looks natural that didn't come off, and you could wear it during all your daily activities. I'm guessing most of you have seen these ads too. I asked my girlfriend at the time what she thought. She said if I wanted to do it to go for it.

At that stage, while my hair had definitely receded, I still had a reasonable amount of my own hair. It had been receding in front and had just started receding on top. I thought if I was going to do this and try a hair system, I wanted to do so when it wouldn't be quite so obvious.

I did my research, talked to people who had done it, and got positive feedback. I decided to give it a shot. I don't think I fully understood what I was committing to.

The hair systems at that time were affixed in one of two ways. They either sewed them on or used glue. Eventually, glue was the only method, as you could feel the stitching, but the glue gave a more natural look and feel. They would typically stay on for about 30 days at a time, and then it was time to go in, get cleaned up, and have them reattached. Otherwise, you treated the system as your normal hair, showering as you usually would and styling it.

My thought was that I'd be completely honest with what I had done and why I had done it. What happened, though, took me a bit by surprise. I purchased a hair system and went in to have it attached. I knew I looked different. I now had a full head of hair. I got back home and went to see my girlfriend. She didn't notice. I was stunned.

When I saw my friends, most didn't react or say anything. Neither did my employees or coworkers. I decided at that time if most people weren't saying anything and my girlfriend didn't even notice initially, I wasn't going to say anything either.

Part of the lack of reaction was that while they might have noticed something was different, I made one change to divert attention. I had a moustache at the time I got the system installed. I shaved it off. The first reaction of some was noticing something was different and then thinking it was that I had shaved off my moustache.

I got reactions from some who told me they clearly recognized the difference. At the same time, I rarely brought it up. My friends who knew me before I had the system were aware. But I never discussed it with those whom I became friends with afterward. I had no idea if they knew it wasn't my real hair.

Even my nieces were unaware. They were then in their teens, and they had only known Uncle Mike with a full head of hair. They didn't know it wasn't my own, and my sister and her husband hadn't told them.

A neighbor of mine who was both a chiropractor and naturopath suggested that the glue in the system could be causing me some of my brain fog issues and could be causing some other significant problems. I felt it was worth exploring and started doing an extensive amount of research, including contacting the manufacturer of the particular glue my stylist used. I couldn't get any definitive proof one way or the other as to whether it was causing me harm. The one thing I did know was that it certainly wasn't helping me.

When I first started wearing a system, shaved heads weren't in. Now they are, and for that, I'm very thankful. I made the decision I was going to take my system off. It was an extremely difficult decision for me. First, I felt at that time that I looked better and younger with it on. Second, and more important to me, I felt like I was disclosing that I was a bit of a fraud or insecure by wearing the hair system. I had now lost most of my hair. Plus, I knew I'd shave my head. The change was going to be extremely obvious. I did decide I was going to add a slight goatee, but that certainly wasn't going to distract anyone from the significant change to the top of my head.

I had debated on the timing. My stylist was great and said she'd help me transition. She said I had a nice head (she was the only one who had seen me without my hair) and that I'd look good with it shaved. She helped me get the equipment I'd need to take care of it myself.

One day I went in and she was going to reaffix the system. It hit me in the moment. I said, "I'm done. Let's shave my head. I don't want to put the system back on."

I was now going to be disclosing to everyone in my life that I had come to know over the past 20 years that my hair wasn't my own. I had absolutely no idea how many people I met during that time knew it wasn't my real hair and had never said anything. It's not something most people bring up. They don't say, "Hey, is that your real hair?"

To me, though, it was the opportunity to be authentic. I had been authentic with everyone about my stress and panic attack issues. Now I could be fully authentic about how I looked too.

There were two possible health benefits. The first was from getting rid of the glue. I can't honestly say I've felt any different without the glue on my head. I just know it wasn't a health benefit to me and could only be a detriment. Second, since I have my heat issues, there was the thought that not wearing the system would keep me cooler. In actuality, I've experienced the opposite. First, if the sun is beating on my head, it's hotter. And it's even warmer if I need to wear a hat. The system breathed and was actually cooler for me than my shaved head with a hat, regardless of the type of hat. It was still warmer for me even if I wore caps that were designed to be lighter or cooler.

Again, I was surprised at the reaction from all those in my life when they first saw me without hair. I did get some strange looks. I also received tremendous support. No one gave me a hard time about wearing a system all those years. Universally, they all said they liked my look better with my shaved head. Personally, I'm torn. I think I prefer the look this way. Regardless, I know I'm very glad I did it and wish I had done it years earlier. It does make me feel more authentic. Now I'll tease myself more than anybody about being bald. I might look a few years older than I did with hair (although some say I look younger now), and I was sensitive about that initially. But I found myself letting go of my insecurities around all that my hair represented to me.

The funny part for me was when I hadn't seen certain people for an extended period of time, and the last time they had seen me was with the hair system. I wouldn't realize they hadn't seen me this way until I saw their expression. It rarely happens anymore, as it's been many years since I've taken my system off. All I could do was smile and say, "I guess it's been a while. You haven't seen me with my new hair style."

Michael Levin

My Lessons Learned

The number one thing for me is the word I've mentioned many times in this chapter: "authenticity." Being authentic with friends, family, employees, and clients about what was going on in my life. Not hiding the issues I was having. Being open about the fact that I didn't have any hair, which seems incredibly trivial compared with the other issues. Yet making that physical change was actually harder for me than sharing the emotional issues.

Universally, the fact that I received such tremendous support was incredibly heartwarming to me. I believe in times like this you find out who your friends are. I feel very fortunate to have such great people in my life. I believe many of us will find that challenging and difficult situations will bring us closer, and the resulting support and trust that is built will provide a great bond.

My lessons and the support I was going to need were going to get more dramatic, as you'll read about in the upcoming chapters. While I was clearly getting lessons that were helping me grow both personally and professionally, I had more to learn.

I've also found that sharing and allowing others to support you doesn't make you weak. I believe it only makes you weak if you become a victim versus trying to do something about it. It doesn't mean that you won't have setbacks in your efforts; I've had many. I personally think you keep on learning and working to improve.

I haven't experienced anyone in my life viewing me as less for what I've been through or what I've disclosed. I think it has helped them feel more comfortable acknowledging their own stuff, whatever those things may be, along with feeling more comfortable asking me for help and support when they need it.

I had a friend who had a physical experience associated with stress when she felt she was unable to be authentic. She was going through a divorce and still living under the same roof with her husband. She had lost her voice for a considerable period of time. They had a very nice home, and neither wanted to move out. At the time, she felt financially dependent on her husband, as she had gone back to school and he was supporting the family. In the past, she had been the primary breadwinner. She finally felt she had to move out regardless of the cost. She'd find a way to pay for the hotel versus feeling like she was being controlled during a difficult time.

She moved into a hotel, and immediately her voice came back. She felt it was because she had lost her voice in the relationship. She felt as though she were in a position of weakness staying under the same roof. Once she took a stand and left, she got her power back, and her voice returned.

I don't think this is unusual. To me, this was a very direct physical/psychological impact. Yet if she went to a doctor to be checked for why she lost her voice, I'm guessing moving out would not have been one of the solutions. I do think it's up to us to explore within ourselves what we might be doing psychologically that can be causing physical symptoms. And if we aren't being true to ourselves—being authentic—then I do believe we give away our power. And there can be a price to pay.

CHAPTER 8

The Blood Is Flowing

I was at a buddy's house for our weekly game night. Our game of choice for some time has been Boggle.

While playing, I felt what seemed like a pizza burn on my tongue. The only problem was, I hadn't had pizza and hadn't done anything to cause anything similar to a pizza burn.

Just before I left, I went into his bathroom. I looked at my tongue, and it was bleeding. It appeared that a sore had opened up. I wasn't overly concerned about it, thought it would stop, and went home.

When I got home, though, I took the situation a lot more seriously. My tongue was bleeding profusely, not only from the sore, but from the crevice in the center of my tongue. I tried putting pressure on it, but I couldn't remotely slow down the blood flow. I got scared and called a friend of mine who was a nurse.

She came over, and between ice and pressure, after about two hours, it finally stopped. We were both at the place where if it didn't stop soon, she was going to take me to the emergency room. We just didn't know what they could do to help.

I went to the doctor the next day, and he noticed my tongue had a yellow coating. He thought the cause was some sort of bacterial infection. He prescribed an antibiotic, and about a week later, my tongue looked almost normal again. I assumed that was the cause of my problem.

About a month later, when taking a shower, I rinsed out my mouth and nothing but blood came out. My tongue was bleeding profusely again. This time, I felt no pizza burn, and there was absolutely no pain either. My tongue was just bleeding. Until I rinsed out my mouth in the shower, I had no idea it was bleeding or that there was any issue.

I went back to the doctor, as my tongue was yellow again. He once more prescribed the antibiotic. This time, my tongue stayed yellow.

I was seeing an acupuncturist, whom I had told about my tongue bleeding. She had noticed the yellow on my tongue. She didn't want to override the doctor's diagnosis the first time but felt compelled to share her beliefs after the second episode.

She said in Chinese medicine, a yellow tongue is a sign the body is retaining heat. She felt this was an internal heat and stress issue. This was occurring during the time my body wasn't sweating. She felt it was all related. She targeted her acupuncture to help me and also started me on some herbs.

In time, my tongue started to look better. It appeared to make a difference. I still notice how the color in my tongue changes. I notice a greater yellowing at times when I am feeling more stress. The crevice also becomes more pronounced.

A third occurrence happened about three months later. I was with my girlfriend, and she said, "Your tongue is bleeding." I had no idea. Again, it was bleeding profusely. Just as before, it took almost two hours to begin to staunch the flow.

A bit of a mass had begun to form on my tongue. I wanted to be sure that the acupuncturist was accurate and there wasn't anything more to this. I went to an ear, nose, and throat specialist. She was concerned when she saw it, as it was unlike anything she had seen. At the same time, she didn't think it was cancerous but wanted to be sure.

She tested it and it came back negative. At the same time, she had no solution to get rid of the mass, nor any idea what caused my tongue to bleed so profusely.

I decided to continue down my path with acupuncture and Chinese herbs. I began taking Qi Gong classes from my acupuncturist. Along with increasing my frequency, I practiced it at home.

I stepped up my therapy to work on the root causes of my issues with stress. In doing so, the mass began to dissipate. It eventually went away. I still see an occasional bump, and the yellowness comes and goes.

I still find all this fascinating—how my body can have such dramatic physical reactions to an emotional and mental issue. To acknowledge this at times can make me feel weak. How am I not strong enough to overcome this?

It can feel like I'm being emotionally fragile. At the same time, I can't deny the physical reactions and the cause. Sucking it up isn't always the solution.

I am also learning that there can be a real power and strength in sharing my vulnerability or "weaknesses." I'm finding that my sharing can help others share and acknowledge their own issues and challenges.

As a man, I feel that such sharing might be even more important, as I think men are frequently raised not to show weakness. We feel we can be perceived as soft. We are told to be tough and that crying is weak.

I remember hearing those words from my father. There was a time I was in our backyard as a youngster and I was in a fight. My father saw the fight. Instead of breaking it up, he said, "This is your problem; finish it." So I did. I was expected to be tough.

As I mentioned earlier, my parents passed away when I was young. My mother died of cancer when I was 16. When I was 18, my father, who I always felt was so tough, performed what can certainly be considered an extreme act of weakness. He committed suicide. He left my sister, who was three years younger than me, and I to fend for ourselves.

I swore I would never be weak like my father was. I would push through this and do what was necessary to ensure my sister and I were OK.

I would not allow my situation to be an excuse for any failures. I would not be reliant on others. My feeling was that many others had been through much worse, and to use it as any kind of excuse was completely unacceptable. I never let go of that attitude.

While that perspective served me extremely well to take care of myself and my sister, it also led me to put undue pressure on myself and adhere to ridiculous standards throughout my life.

I felt I could be compassionate and supportive to others. While I didn't tolerate excuses in others or accept someone being a "victim," I believe my friends have always felt they could come to me and talk to me, and I'd be there for them and support them.

On the flip side, I wasn't very compassionate to myself. I wouldn't take care of myself. I felt being self-sufficient, eating pretty healthy, and exercising was enough. I didn't want to lean on or ask for help from others. I didn't want to feel needy in any way. It was difficult for me to let others support or take care of me, even when they wanted to.

I frequently travel for both business and pleasure. I was on the tail end of back-to-back business trips. My girlfriend offered to wash my clothes for me from the prior trip. I am perfectly capable of washing my own clothes. I've been doing so since I was nine. When I stepped back and understood what was going on, I realized she really wanted to support me when I was busy traveling. It was a way she could show how much she cared for me and loved me. She wasn't doing it just to be nice. She offered because she really wanted to, and I needed to accept her act of kindness. I brought my clothes over. Her response was, "Is that all you have?" She wanted to do more. I am still learning how to accept acts of kindness, even if they are things I am more than capable of doing for myself.

Michael Levin

My Lessons Learned

As I'm writing this chapter, I'm coming back from a combination business/pleasure trip. I had a client engagement in New York City with an associate of mine teaching presentation skills. After the three-day workshop, I decided to take a couple of days to make the lengthy drives first to Cooperstown to see the Baseball Hall of Fame and then to Niagara Falls. Both were bucket-list items for me.

The trip was a bit stressful. We had some challenges regarding class logistics, and my associate was stressed. I found it rubbing off on me. I also had felt more personal stress around some client engagements coming into the week. In Cooperstown, I was in the shower and noticed a tinge of red when I rinsed my mouth out. I looked at my tongue when I got out of the shower, and the crevice was redder and had a spot or two of blood on it. Nothing like what I had experienced before with profuse bleeding. But clearly my tongue was sending me a message.

I also had been feeling more stressed in general, as I had a long-term contract come to a conclusion, and although I'm in great shape financially, I was feeling a bit of stress that my outflow was temporarily going to be exceeding my income, especially with some business investments I wanted to make. The combination of everything I noticed was causing some physical reactions for me.

The next day at Niagara Falls was quite warm for me: 86 and muggy. Near the falls was cooler, between the breeze and water. Away from it, I was feeling the effects much quicker than usual. That also gave me a clear message: my body was stressed. Normally, I would push through this because I'd never know when or if I'd get back to Niagara Falls. And I thought it was spectacular.

I decided to take a break. I went in and had some lunch. I cooled down. I did some self-talk and deep breathing. I wanted to relax into the day, enjoy my time, free my body of stress, and just enjoy whatever I could of Niagara Falls. I wasn't going to push myself. If I went out and had problems with the heat, I'd call it a day and be grateful for what I did experience.

I ended up having a great afternoon. I didn't have any more problems with the heat. I felt well enough to go on a boat tour that took us up next to the falls. It was incredible, and we got soaked. The tour guides warned us it could be warm before we got on the boat, especially if we put on the rain jackets they had given us (which were definitely needed). I didn't have any problems at all.

The next part I am sharing is candidly quite hard for me to do. As I said at the start, this isn't about what I've accomplished; it's about what I've learned and am continuing to learn daily. The learning continues as I'm writing this book and will long after I've finished it.

I have felt, with regard to all my issues, that I've made progress and haven't backslid significantly on any of them. I have now found out that isn't true. I admit that writing what I'm about to share next affected me briefly from a credibility standpoint. I also feel I would be less than authentic without full disclosure. If I'm asking you to benefit from what I've learned, part of it is not beating yourself up when you backslide but instead learning from it and make changes.

I had stopped a couple of the components of my healing process. I haven't done any of my meditational practices recently, such as Qi Gong. I had stopped taking my herbs. I hadn't done any acupuncture. I budget a certain amount each month for taking care of myself from a more holistic standpoint, such as through chiropractic, massage, Rolfing, acupuncture, and so on. I also had suffered some injuries and was trying to get them resolved. Acupuncture fell further down my list as to what I felt my body needed.

On Monday, when I returned to California, I was out with a friend at a sports bar watching the Golden State Warriors basketball playoff game. I felt a bit of a salty taste on my tongue and had a bad feeling. I dabbed it with a napkin, and my tongue was bleeding. Not just a little bit this time, but badly.

I had felt this would never occur again. Now, looking at my habits, I was doing things to "stay fit." I was eating pretty healthy, working out, and doing well for the most part at getting a good night's sleep. But I still wasn't doing all I needed to do to "stay in shape."

I told my friend we'd need to finish watching the game at my house. I didn't feel any panic around it. And there was no pain. My tongue just bled profusely. If I hadn't noticed the salty taste on my tongue, I wouldn't have been aware.

This ended up being my longest bout of not being able to stop the bleeding. I kept ice and pressure on it, and it still bled profusely for more than three hours. I was at the stage of going to the emergency room, which I had never done before. I wasn't sure how much blood I lost or how quickly it was being replenished. I gave myself a deadline. I wasn't sure what they could do for me in emergency, but if I couldn't stop it myself, I had to try another alternative.

Finally, about 15 minutes before my self-imposed deadline, I was able to get the bleeding to stop. I made a vow to get back on track with the things that helped me in the first place. I've started doing Qi Gong again. My goal is minimally twice per week. I'm going back to the acupuncturist. I've started taking the herbs that had helped me before.

Personally, I also needed to set boundaries too. With my associate, I couldn't let her stress rub off on me. We had a conversation about it, and I was very candid with her. My associate is an outstanding trainer as well as a good friend. She can also get very stressed if things don't go as planned.

I told her if she was stressed, I could hear it once. After that, I was happy to help support her with a solution. I wasn't open to her stress reaction on multiple occasions for the same issue. She heard me, and her response to both understanding and supporting my need were all I could ask for.

I have learned (and am still learning) to ask for my needs to be met. My tendency has been to strictly look inward and do what I could to make things better. I still do that. I've gotten much better, though, at asking for support for my needs from others as well. And I feel good that I can do so calmly, exploring a solution that's good for everyone involved.

I guess sometimes you have to take a step backward to go forward. This was a backward step for me. I also needed to not beat myself up too badly for this. I definitely did for a bit in this case, as I felt like, especially in writing this book, that I was setting a poor example. I've got to realize I'm human too, and I'm going to make mistakes or backslide on habits and lifestyle changes. I just need to learn from them and go forward. This is a journey, isn't it?

CHAPTER 9

The Harshest Lesson Yet

I felt I had gotten some pretty strong messages that I needed to take care of myself. From the damage I created due to stress from my health issues—my body not being able to handle heat and not sweating and my tongue bleeding profusely—I thought I was getting the message. I was about to find out that my loudest and strongest message was yet to come. I still had more to learn.

I continue to work though the wake-up call I am about to share with you. And as a result, another message hit me. This may sound a bit odd, but it's one of the reasons I'm writing this book. I felt like I could have gotten the point with potentially less harsh messages. And I began to feel it was a bit selfish to think these messages were only designed to help *me*. I came to the realization that I was supposed to share what I was going through and learning in order to help others. Again, it wasn't about sharing what I've overcome. I felt I needed to share the knowledge that I've gained to help others who might be experiencing reactions to stress and, like me, might not realize the cause or what to do about it.

As I share my next message with you, I'll also tell you this one is a bit more graphic. I feel it's important to tell this story openly as I can, because I believe it may lose some impact if I don't. This health issue was certainly the most difficult to be open about.

I had a feeling something was off when I went to the bathroom, as I had been having a burning sensation for some time. I anticipated I might have a prostate issue. I went for my annual physical, and my prostate specific antigen, or PSA, was high. My doctor sent me to a urologist. I wasn't overly worried because I thought if I did have prostate cancer, we were catching it early, and I had been told prostate cancer was slow growing. What the doctor discovered, I would never have imagined.

When I had my appointment, the urologist had me get on the table and did a scan. After the scan, he gave me a strange look. He asked me if I needed to go to the bathroom. I said no, that I went just before my appointment. He said, "You've got two liters of urine in your bladder. We need to catheterize you immediately."

I went back to the bathroom to try to go again. Very little came out. Now, for me personally, I had been catheterized twice before. As an athlete, I've suffered more injuries than I can count, including a dislocated shoulder and broken ribs. For me, easily the most painful experience of my life was being catheterized.

The urologist inserted the catheter, and he was right. Two liters came out. I was blown away. He said this wasn't something new. This was a long-term problem that he couldn't determine the origin of. But the good news was that I hadn't suffered any kidney damage, which could have easily occurred. However, this was also not a situation I could live with. My bladder showed considerable scarring and was badly damaged. He said I was going to have to start self-catheterizing immediately several times a day.

He had me try to practice, and the pain brought me to my knees. I couldn't do it. I asked him if he could give me a week to see if I could get this solved on my own through holistic methods. He said that was fine.

As far as I had known, I went to the bathroom like everybody else. I had no idea I had this problem. Over the next week, it seemed to me like I was going to the bathroom just fine. I got some more holistic treatments, from massage to acupuncture. The next week, I went back hoping things were better.

They weren't. They were worse. They catheterized me again that day. The urologist said he only had two long-term solutions for me: I could learn how to self-catheterize, or he could surgically implant an external valve that fed into my bladder. I could insert a tube into the valve and use that to go to the bathroom.

I couldn't imagine either solution. Self-catheterization I felt wasn't an option. I was also single at the time and always felt that for a woman to want to be in a relationship with me, I had to be strong and as perfect for her as possible. Faults, physical or otherwise, could turn women off, and they wouldn't be interested in me. I couldn't imagine a woman wanting to be with me if I had a permanent valve surgically implanted in my bladder. How could she possibly be attracted to me? Clearly, this was a personal self-acceptance issue I needed to work on.

The urologist wanted to send me to a specialist at Stanford to explore other possible solutions. In the interim, if I wasn't going to self-catheterize, he told me he'd need to insert a catheter that would remain in until either I chose one of the two options he offered or the specialist came up with another possible solution. I asked what my life would be like wearing the catheter, and he felt I could do what I normally did. I'm guessing this urologist has never been catheterized or certainly hadn't had to keep one inserted. I know the urologist he connected me with at Stanford had never been catheterized, because he had admitted that to me.

For me, doing things normally wasn't even remotely an option. I was in constant pain. In the first week, I dropped 10 pounds. I dropped another 15 in the next couple of weeks. I literally looked gray. I was essentially bedridden. I found movement to be extremely painful.

I was no longer going to be able to "suck it up." I had to share my situation with my clients and staff. Even a simple act like going to the grocery store was excruciating and exhausting. Movement would cause me to bleed around the catheter. I couldn't support my clients the way I was used to. When it was possible, my clients were so gracious and insisted I work from home and do what I could. Other activities we postponed until I was in a better place.

My staff was in the same situation. I wasn't coming into the office. I was accessible by phone and e-mail, but aside from that, they were on their own.

I also learned I was going to need support and help from others. Friends would tease me about how I was frequently friends with ex-girlfriends. I typically haven't experienced bitter breakups. In this case, I was extremely grateful for that. Two of them were nurses. One came with me to all my doctor appointments as my advocate and support. Another who lived near me came over every other day to help take care of me and to try to ensure I didn't get any infections. I was also very thankful their new significant others were both understanding and secure.

My friends all stepped up and did whatever they could to support me. One friend gave me an incredibly powerful message. He said, "The only way I will be angry is if you could have used my help and you didn't ask." Those I didn't ask were disappointed I didn't give them the chance to help. It really touched me.

When I initially agreed to the catheter, although I know I didn't have much of a choice, I thought it would be for a few weeks. It turned out that I lived with it for more than three months.

The specialist at Stanford was incredible. He said there were a couple of possible options. There were no guarantees on any of them. I was researching all possible solutions so I could be well informed.

I was still hoping I could solve this naturally. About two months in, as we were exploring possible solutions, the specialist ran some tests. There was some hope as well that wearing the catheter would allow my bladder to self-heal to some extent, and things would start working naturally. I had hoped that between that and my holistic efforts of acupuncture, therapy, massage, meditation, and personal growth books I was reading, my problem would be solved.

You could be asking yourself, "How does this situation relate to stress, and how did stress cause this? It sounds like a legitimate physical issue."

I believe it is a legitimate physical issue as well as one involving stress. I don't believe it has to be all one way or another. They can cross lines. I think stress can exacerbate physical issues.

The doctors had no idea what caused my condition in the first place. I do feel this started as a physical issue and was then exacerbated by stress. The fact that I was so out of touch with my body and couldn't even feel that I had two liters inside me told me a lot. If you can imagine two liters of liquid in your bladder and not feeling a desire or need to go, that's what I was experiencing.

It was interesting getting varied opinions from the Eastern and Western communities. I asked the Western doctors if they felt my urine retention and my heat issue could be related. They all felt it wasn't. The Eastern or holistic practitioners I saw felt the opposite: the theme that I was both retaining heat (not sweating) and retaining urine were tied together. I personally believe they are correct and that there is at least some connection between the two.

Without a doubt, though, I was learning very important lessons that have significantly changed how I live and how I can help others. They are lifetime changes that provide a daily reminder of how I need to take care of myself. Now back to my story.

I thought I was doing so much better. My color had begun to return. My weight was still down 20 pounds, but I looked and felt dramatically better. As I put it, the catheter and I had made friends.

I knew I looked bad, but I'm not sure I realized how bad I appeared to others. I had become very frail. My nieces were used to their uncle who had energy and always wanted to play with them. It actually scared them to see me. When I started looking better and saw friends who hadn't seen me at my worst, they were still stunned as to how bad I looked. I had to laugh, as they had no idea what an improvement my current appearance was.

I went to Stanford for some tests. The urologist hooked me up to some elaborate equipment. His goal was to see if I had made any improvement and to measure what functionality, if any, I had in my bladder. He wanted to see if I was a candidate for any of the possible procedures he had in mind. I was nervous, but I was optimistic.

They put a number of probes on me and set me up to try to go to the bathroom. I could barely go. Some came out, but not nearly all I had in me. I was angry and frustrated. I felt like I had been working so hard.

I was hopeful I was going to be able to go on my own and everything would be normal again. I wanted the catheter out very badly.

The urologist came in and met with me. He said that obviously the catheter would have to go back in. The good news was that their tests showed some minor functionality. I was a candidate for their options. The first option was a prostate resection. He asked me if I wanted children. I told him no. He said, "Good, because in all likelihood, the surgery would leave you incapable."

He scheduled the surgery a few weeks out. I asked him what would happen if it didn't work. I had been doing a lot of research myself and was aware of other potential options. One was inserting electrical stimuli into the bladder. He said if the prostate resection didn't work, they'd reinsert the catheter. I'd need to give it another three months and they would try one of the other options. I couldn't imagine the catheter staying in that long.

I asked him what the odds were of this working. He was pretty optimistic. He felt there was up to an 80 percent chance I'd have some success with this surgery.

During this time, I had been running my businesses from my home. I had made the drive one day to our Santa Cruz office just to see my staff. I clearly didn't look remotely like I did when they saw me last, and with the catheter in me, I was moving extremely slowly.

It was great to see them. They were so supportive. They had stepped up during this time and had done a great job. It showed me a lot that I could entrust not only my friends but my staff to step up when I needed them. All they had from me was the occasional phone call and e-mail support. And it was all they needed.

My style of leadership is to create ownership and independence from my staff. I want my staff to be entrepreneurial. It's what I've always tried to manifest in my companies, and I find it works very well. It's at times like this, though, when it tells me so much more. To me, it was a combination of them truly taking ownership when I most needed them to and a degree of loyalty and respect to be there when I needed them most. There was also an understanding on their part that I needed to take care of myself and was doing all I could do. I hold my teams to what I believe is a high standard, and that includes showing up for work every day. I hadn't been there for almost three months. But none of them took advantage of it. They just supported me.

This was a very interesting time for me in other ways that tested what brought on the stress in the first place. I changed my lifestyle dramatically during this time, much out of necessity. I made sure I slept well. I've always set an alarm on workdays and still do. During this time, I didn't. I woke up when I woke up. Typically, it was still no later than 7:30, and I was working by 8:30. I wanted to let my body heal as much as possible.

As I mentioned earlier in the book, I can stress about money. Financially, I was doing great. At the same time, it was very hard for me to walk away from business. I had to turn down client requests and ask if we could delay until I was better. Overall, they were very understanding. One of the toughest things to turn down was a class an associate of mine and I teach called "Presenting Powerfully." It's her workshop, and years ago, she asked me if I would coteach it with her. She teaches the curriculum, and I conduct private coaching sessions for the attendees.

We had a workshop coming up at Clorox. It triggered me on several levels. First, it affected my stress because of the possibility of giving up current and future income. Second, when I make a commitment, I don't want to let anyone down. I felt I could potentially push through and coach the attendees. I knew if I said no, my associate would need to find someone else for that workshop. The person she would use had badly wanted my role. I was concerned about not only giving up the workshop but whether my associate would want to work with this other person going forward. She said that wouldn't be the case, yet the idea still played with me.

When I talked with my therapist about it, she said, "You can do the workshop. But at what price?" I completely agreed. I felt what she said made a lot of sense. I needed to work through my insecurities and typical areas of stress and take care of myself. I turned the workshop down. Now, three years later, my associate and I still work together, typically about a dozen times a year, teaching that workshop. We are told consistently by our clients that it's their favorite. I don't know what the impact would have been if I had tried to push through that one time instead of letting go and trusting the future would work out just fine.

The time was coming for my surgery. I felt like I had been doing all I could to help the surgery be successful. I met with the doctor before the surgery. Leading up to that day, I had asked him a ton of questions. I felt like I might have been a complainer. He had a more accurate perspective. He said, "You aren't a complainer. You are a worrier." That was quite accurate. It was something I needed to look at, as the worrying wasn't serving me.

He also said something else that was very important. He said I wasn't a number. He said he'd be there to help me. He also didn't want me to stress about how much I went to the bathroom postsurgery. He only wanted me to be able to go. He knew my tendency would be to stress and measure how much I took in and how much came out to see if I was retaining. He wanted me to relax around it, not stress, and just focus on being able to go, not how much.

After the surgery, my doctor said it went well. He was optimistic. The catheter had been reinserted. He wanted it in for another three days to let me heal. At the end of three days, it could come out. I'd then have about five hours for my body to start working and be able to go to the bathroom.

I reached out to a good buddy of mine, Curt, for his support. He was the one who told me that if I could use his help, he'd only be upset if I didn't ask. I asked him if he'd take the day off when I got the catheter out and if he'd hang out with me. Ideally, he'd just be there to keep me company. At worst, he'd need to take me back to the hospital to have the catheter reinserted.

Michael Levin

That evening, after the surgery, I felt fine. The catheter was back in. I had dinner with a friend. I took it easy for the next couple of days. Then the day came. I was going to find out if the surgery worked, at least to some degree. The final verdict wouldn't come for another couple of days, when I'd go back in to be scanned to see if I was retaining any urine.

That morning, my ex-girlfriend, the nurse that lived near me, came over and took the catheter out. I went for some bodywork to help me relax. Curt came over later that morning to hang out with me.

It felt great to have the catheter out. It was the first time in months I was able to walk around without a catheter inserted and a bag attached to my leg. There was no way I wanted the catheter back in.

About three hours had passed and nothing was happening. I was trying to stay calm and felt like I was doing a pretty good job of it. Curt and I talked about anything and everything to keep my mind off it. I just wanted to feel the urge and go.

I asked him if he minded if we walked around the neighborhood. I was hoping movement might help. It was now nearing the four-hour mark. I had been instructed I should come back in at the five-hour mark. I felt I might push it a little bit.

As we were walking, I felt the urge come on. I told Curt he needed to excuse me for a minute. I wanted to see if I could go and didn't want to wait and try to hold it in until we got back home.

I started trying to push to see if I could go. Things started to work. I had no idea how I'd feel. More than anything, I felt relieved. No pun intended; it was how I felt. Not elation. Not joy. Just relief. I had no idea if I went completely or partially. I was thankful I was able to go and, at least for the moment, the catheter wasn't going back in.

Over the next few days, I was able to go slowly but steadily. I still didn't know if it was enough and if I was voiding completely. The day had come to get scanned and find out how well the surgery had worked.

That night had been rough. I hadn't gone all night. I was in a lot of pain. My ex-girlfriend thought I might have a stricture creating a blockage that might need to be opened up. That day, prior to the scan, I hardly went.

I was having flashbacks to the scan in which the doctor found two liters of urine inside me. When I went in for the appointment, I told the doctor about what was going on. I told him there was no way I wanted the catheter going back in. If I was retaining, I wanted to check for a blockage or stricture.

The doctor and his nurse wanted me to go and do the best I could. I came back in for the scan. I had no idea what to expect. The doctor stepped out, and the nurse conducted the scan.

She told me there was only one ounce inside me! That's when the emotions came up for me. I'm not someone who cries, but that news brought tears to my eyes. I gave the nurse a huge hug. I could tell she thought I must be crazy. I was so excited. I felt like I had my life back!

The doctor came back in. He said, despite the pain I felt, he didn't believe I had any clots or strictures. He thought I was doing great. In fact, he was stunned I was doing so well.

When he said that, I was surprised. I told him I thought he was confident it would work. He had been confident, but he thought I'd continue to retain, but at a safer level. He never expected me to be able to void so completely, not with the level of functionality I had.

His words made me feel good for several reasons. The obvious one was that I was doing so well. I was in the clear, at least for now. Another big one was that I had felt a significant amount of frustration that I needed surgery and I hadn't been able to fix the problem naturally. What became apparent to me was that all the work I had done on myself *had* made a real difference. Without all the work, I might have had no functionality and the surgery wouldn't have been possible. The work helped me achieve results that stunned my doctor, and I was able to perform to a much higher level than my limited function should have allowed.

Things certainly aren't normal. It's still hard for me to go. It takes a lot of effort. Standing up to go is no longer possible. But things work. I am thankful every day. I don't take it for granted.

I also know I have to take care of myself. I can't put any undue strain or pressure on my bladder. I go regularly whether I feel the need or not. For an extended period of time, I'd set my alarm at night so my body would get used to waking me up if I needed to go. Now I no longer need an alarm. I minimize my fluid intake at night, and my body wakes up on its own if it needs to.

About a year after the surgery, I started having problems again. There was pain when I went to the bathroom. I noticed it was getting harder to go. I was still going, but I knew something was wrong.

I met with the doctor, and he said they'd need to go back inside with a catheter to look at what was going on. Clearly, I was very resistant at the thought. He said he was sorry, but it was necessary. As always, I found the procedure to be extremely painful.

As he inserted the catheter, he told me I should look at the monitor. I said no, that I just wanted to breathe and keep my eyes closed to try to take my mind off the pain. He told me again he thought I should look at the monitor, so I did. I could see what looked like teeth. Even to an untrained eye, I could see that I had blockages. It was the reason for my pain and why things had gotten more difficult. I was relieved that was the issue.

The doctor said I would need another surgery. He would need to take out the blockages. I was totally fine with it.

The surgery came and went. This time, I went back postsurgery a few days later, and he took the catheter out. He did a test immediately, inserting a significant amount of water before the catheter came out. He wanted to know if the surgery worked. And it did. Unlike the first surgery, I felt confident that things would work. This surgery actually made things even easier than the first. While I still can't stand up to go, it is much better.

I know there might be more surgeries in my future. There literally isn't a day that goes by that I'm not grateful for doing something that most of us take for granted. Regardless of where I am—at home, with a client, at a ballgame, or on an airplane—I do whatever I need to do to take care of myself. It is a daily reminder that I can do what I need to do to take care of and support myself without sacrificing the needs of others and taking care of them as well.

My Lessons Learned

Before my first surgery, my therapist asked if I would come to her office. She had something she wanted to try and needed it to be in person. Our sessions had been over the phone since I had been wearing the catheter. Her office was an hour from my house. It was a long trip for me, and I knew I'd have to walk a little bit, as there was no parking next to her office. It would only be about two blocks. Two blocks, at this stage, could be extremely difficult for me. What I didn't know at the time was that my biggest lesson was going to come before my session, not during. This I remember vividly. I honestly can't recall what we did in the session. I wrote in my journal that the session was helpful, but I wasn't specific as to what it was.

I drove over to her office and parked as close as I could. It was still going to be a two-block walk from one of the city's parking lots. I was in a great deal of pain walking. Every step was difficult. I was bleeding quite a bit, and frankly, it was making me feel both angry and sorry for myself. It was only a short two-block walk, but it may as well have been 10 miles. I kept stopping to catch my breath and let the pain subside.

A little over halfway to her office, I noticed an older man. He appeared to be bleeding through his nose. I walked up to him to see if I could help and noticed he was bleeding from several places, some pretty heavily, as he must have fallen and gotten back up. He was extremely disoriented. About the same time, a tow truck driver noticed as well and came over to help. He had a first-aid kit on his truck.

He had his staff call 9-1-1 and brought the first-aid kit over. We pulled cloths out to try to stop the bleeding. I walked over to a nearby store and asked if we could borrow a chair so I could take it back to the man and let him sit down. We didn't want him falling over.

It turned out his name was William. He was 87 years old. He was out with his son, and they had separated for some reason. His son found us and immediately panicked. The tow truck driver and I told him to go get some ice, as his panicking wasn't helping his father.

During this time, I completely forgot about my own pain. While I had been shuffling extremely slowly before I saw William, I moved quickly and without pain to help William and get him a chair. I know it was adrenaline. At the same time, I also know it was so much more.

Both the tow truck driver and I had remained calm throughout the incident and helped keep William calm. We waited until the ambulance arrived. Up until then, I was having a pity party. I received a very clear message. I don't think it was an accident that I was the one to find William. I think I was meant to help him. He helped heal me more than I helped heal him. It was my reminder that regardless of whether things are bad, there are people who have it much worse. I'm very lucky.

When I talk about my harsh messages, while they certainly have been difficult, they are more unique than anything else. I haven't had a heart attack or stroke from stress as others have. I don't have a disease that is incurable. I'm having challenges I need to work through and take ownership of, and I do the best I can to take care of myself.

I was grateful for the chance to help William. I was also grateful for the message that was sent to me. I might not have gotten it otherwise.

At the request of my therapist, I had begun journaling in April of 2012. This period of my life with regards to the catheter began in July of 2012. My journal is 43 pages long. Of the 43 pages in my journal, only 15 pages are before the surgery. I actually wrote an additional 28 pages in my journal after the surgery.

I'm proud of that. My normal tendency would be to go back to my old habits once things got back to normal. This time I continued to do as my therapist asked. I didn't backslide as I normally would. Until I looked back in my notes while writing this book, I didn't realize this.

It is a reminder of a lesson learned. It's too easy to backslide into old habits. They might be daily habits of things we do or emotional habits of things we worry about, stress about, or put too much energy toward.

Continuing to journal was a very good habit for me. While I don't journal now and don't feel the need, it's a reminder for me to continue with other positive habits. My tendency, as my brother-in-law said, is to stay fit. I'm committed to working out. I do a decent job of staying in shape physically. But I also need to stay in shape mentally. That means doing Qi Gong, doing the things I need to do to destress, and not putting energy toward things that don't add value or are a waste of time.

From what I understand, we have 60,000 to 90,000 thoughts per day. Of those thoughts, up to 80 percent can be negative. It's where we go. I think it's why in a work atmosphere it can be much more "fun" to gossip about negative things than to be positive and try to find solutions to issues or figure out ways to make things better. I know I can get caught up in the same thing—thinking about things I can't control or issues I shouldn't be putting energy toward. I need to remain positive, thankful, and grateful. I am very lucky.

CHAPTER 10

Lessons Learned

I was so grateful to have my life back. I knew I had to make a number of changes. It was interesting to me that my sweating issue, while still something I wanted to improve, held less importance to me. The thought of a valve implanted had far greater repercussions. I do know at some point in time that could still happen. I'm also going to do all I can for that never to occur. And if it does, I'll be fine.

For me, there is a self-acceptance that came with what I've gone through. I need to ask those in my life to accommodate me because I can't be out when it's too hot. I like to golf, and my friends know either we have to play when it's cooler or sometimes I might need to cancel if it's a hot day.

I had to learn that I didn't need to be perfect or free of flaws to attract someone in my life. I've had a lot of relationships over the years and lived with two women long term. While I have been with wonderful women over the years, it has been challenging to end up in the right relationship whether by my choice, theirs, or both of ours. I had retained this feeling that I needed to be free of flaws. It wasn't something the women I've been with had said. This was my message to myself. And it wasn't an accurate one.

I didn't care about any—for lack of better terms—flaws or quirks in others. I normally found them endearing. It wasn't as if I expected that in someone else. I just expected flawlessness in myself.

What I have gone through has helped me understand that women will not only accept my flaws; they can find them endearing as well. As I'm writing this chapter, I'm sitting next to my fiancée, Joanna. We're on a weekend getaway, staying at her aunt's beach house in Aptos, California. I told her what I was writing about and asked her how she would feel if I ever had to have a valve implanted.

She gave me the answer I knew she would. She wouldn't care. She said she loved me unconditionally. She said she'd support me regardless of what I went through. I feel exactly the same about her. We take care of each other. While I'm sure the insecurities may be in the back of my mind, they certainly are no longer in the forefront.

After the surgery, I knew I had to change my lifestyle. I hadn't been able to exercise for three months. I started by walking my neighborhood. My neighborhood is quite hilly. It's not easy to walk. The neighborhood is essentially two large circles, and there are roads off each of the circles. Initially, it was extremely hard, and I'd have to stop several times just to make one lap around one of the circles.

Michael Levin

On those walks, I got back into my habits. I wanted to use the time as productively as possible, so I'd try to catch up on phone calls. Like so many of us, I have a tendency to always be "connected" in some way.

But I decided I wanted to smell the roses, so I started leaving the phone behind on my walks. My neighborhood is beautiful. To the west are rolling hills. There can be wildlife from cows, to horses, to deer, to foxes, to turkeys. To the east is Mount Diablo. It stands high above the rest of the area and has a majestic feel to it.

I started taking the time to enjoy my neighborhood, appreciate the view, and experience the walk. Sometimes I can be lost in my thoughts, as it gives me a chance to "be" versus "do." Since then, I haven't taken the phone with me. It was a boundary I wanted to set up for myself. Walking the neighborhood would be therapeutic both physically and emotionally.

I wanted to balance my workouts as well between the gym, my neighborhood walks, and Qi Gong. I know how easy it is to get too busy to take care of ourselves. At the same time, we take care of our houses, our cars, and our stuff, yet I think we frequently can neglect ourselves. I had read in a magazine about someone who worked out five times a week, and it amounted to 4 percent of his time. It didn't seem like too much to me to give 4 percent of my time to taking care of myself.

I also changed my philosophy about working out. It goes back to my brother-in-law's comment about being fit versus being in shape. I was fit, and I focused more on my external appearance in my gym workouts. I shifted and decided to focus more on being in shape on the inside than fit in appearance on the outside. I stepped up my aerobic workouts to take care of my heart. And I don't sacrifice my meditational workout in Qi Gong to go to the gym.

I came to realize through therapy that I had felt an inordinate level of responsibility to make sure my sister and I were taken care of after our father died. She was overseas in Belgium at the time as an exchange student. I told her to stay and finish out her year, as there was nothing I needed her help for. She was better off being there.

My therapist said what I did at the time was what I needed to do to take care of myself. I couldn't spend too much time feeling sorry for myself. I needed to be sure we were OK. What I learned was I never allowed myself to let go of that inordinate level of responsibility, even after I no longer needed to. I was not going to be like my father and not be around for those I care for. I lived life like I had to support and take care of a family of 10, even though I only needed to take care of myself and be there for my friends and family. It was time to let that go.

I know I've been sharing lessons as we've gone along in this book. I continue to learn, as I sometimes make progress and sometimes take a step back.

When I do find what I've learned helps others, it is incredibly rewarding. While I certainly don't want any more harsh messages, if what I've been through helps somebody else, it makes this journey even more worthwhile.

CHAPTER 11

Books from Heaven?

This whole experience has been somewhat spiritual. It's caused me to look within versus outside for solutions and how to make myself better as well as be better for others. While I'm not religious, I do feel as though I have a spiritual side.

I had an odd experience during this time that I still can't explain. I do feel there was a reason for this experience as part of my journey. It was a bit surreal, and at the same time, there probably is a logical explanation; I just have absolutely no idea what it is.

I opened my front door one day, and there was a package on my porch. It looked like a box you might get from someplace like Amazon. However, there was no return address on it or any postage. When I opened the box, it was a book about Jews for Jesus. I am Jewish by heritage, but I've never followed the religion. What I know for sure is that none of my friends or no one I can possibly think of would send me a book like this. It definitely didn't come from any of my neighbors.

The interesting message for me from this book came some time later, when a very good buddy of mine, Mark, who is a devout Christian, told me he shared my story with his prayer group. It was right before my surgery. Mark refers to me as the Jewish brother he never had, and I feel the same in reverse about him.

He told me there were 5,000 Christians praying for me. It really touched me, as I am a big believer that things like a difference in religious beliefs shouldn't impact how we are with each other, and we should be free of judgment. I was grateful for their prayers. It meant a lot that even though I wasn't part of their faith or prayer group, I was part of their prayers. And they were doing so without any pretense of trying to convert me. They were there simply to provide me support.

The book I received didn't hit my reading list. I still found it incredibly odd and couldn't think of who would possibly send it to me or how they managed to ship a book without any trace as to where it came from.

A couple weeks later, another box showed up on my doorstep. This box had the same characteristics. It looked like a typical shipping box and had a shipping label addressed to me. Yet there was no return address and no postage.

This time it was a book by Wayne Dyer. I knew who he was but knew nothing about him. I had never read anything he had written and had never seen or heard him speak. This book did make it onto my reading list, and I found this book to very compelling. It was a very spiritual book. It surprised me, as I always thought of him as being motivational, and I found this book to be somewhat dry. At the same time, I appreciated much of his message.

The key lesson I got from his book was the power of self-affirmations. And it wasn't only self-affirmations; it was how you said them. He referred to stating those affirmations in the present tense instead of the future tense. For example, instead of saying, "I want to be healthy," you would say, "I am healthy."

This is something I've incorporated into my daily life. I give myself these self-affirmations every night as I'm about to go to sleep. I can't tell you that I can define the impact, but I know it certainly doesn't hurt. I believe it puts your mind in a much more positive place. It helps reaffirm what is important to you and reminds you to put these things in your life now. Saying "I want" means you don't have it. But by putting self-affirmations in the present tense, you are saying that these things *are* in your life now.

As I said, I have no idea where these books came from. No one has ever come forward. I still don't know how someone managed to deliver two books to my front door with a professional shipping label with no return address and no postage. There are friends of mine who are religious who have their own perspective as to how they could have arrived. They felt God's post office doesn't charge postage, and the return address is a bit ethereal. And I also am pretty confident those friends weren't the messengers.

I do know one thing: it certainly wasn't an accident that I got them. And I appreciate the message they delivered.

CHAPTER 12

Helping Others

I feel that what I have learned, what I have been through, and what I can offer are meant to be shared. It has actually felt selfish to me to keep my lessons to myself. Why should other people suffer because they don't understand what's going on with them, just as I didn't understand what was happening to me?

When I've been able to make a difference for someone else, it has meant a tremendous amount to me. The only thing I've asked of others is to pay it forward—to share with others and help them.

I want to share two stories about helping others. My favorite story I alluded to in the introduction of this book. It's about my friend Chris and his wife, Erika.

We were coming back from a guy's baseball weekend in San Diego. There were 12 of us hanging out. Chris used to work for me in a former business of mine. I've always really liked Chris. We hadn't had a lot of deep conversations though.

We were flying back to San Francisco, and Chris and I were sitting next to each other. He was telling me

Michael Levin

about how badly he and his wife wanted to have children. They both had siblings, and they were the only ones who didn't have children. They were in their late 30s and felt they were running out of time.

They had tried all medical possibilities they could. Their doctor had told them they'd never be able to have children. Despite the doctor's words, they hadn't given up hope and were still open to whatever they could explore. I asked Chris if he ever considered the possibility of how stress was impacting their situation. He said he hadn't.

It seemed possible to me, with the amount of pressure they felt because they wanted children so badly, that their bodies could contract. That contraction could prevent the ability of the natural flow necessary for conception to occur. I have no idea if what I'm saying is absolute crap or not. It intuitively felt viable to me that stress could prevent what happens naturally.

I also knew of others who had this experience. When they had taken the pressure off, stopped worrying about having a child, adopted a child, or stopped taking any sort of medication, they had children. I told Chris to talk to a friend of ours, Mark, who had a similar experience and had his first child when he and his wife, Monica, stopped trying.

We talked about different things they could try, and he said he was going to talk to his wife. He was excited, as he felt there might be some hope.

About six months later, Chris reached out to me. He said he had some incredible news. His wife's family is very tight. His wife's sister said she'd be willing to be a surrogate for them. Doctors had said it wouldn't work, but she was open to trying.

It turned out it did work! She was pregnant. They were going to have a baby. And Chris had more news. His wife was also pregnant! She got pregnant one month after her sister.

They had two baby girls, Jasmine and Valeria, who ended up being born 11 days apart.

He shared with me that they had taken my advice to heart. Instead of seeking additional medical help, they treated their situation as emotional, not physical. And by doing so, by addressing it in that way, they proved the doctors wrong. It wasn't a medical issue. It was something they needed to solve themselves, not with a pill.

Chris's story was the most poignant for me, but it was certainly not the only one. My friend Mark, whom I referred to earlier in this chapter, had his own stories. His first story occurred more than 20 years ago when he and his wife had their own childbirth miracle. He also got to personally experience the physical effects of stress himself many years later.

Mark had a very successful business. During the economic downturn, his business began to really struggle. It was an incredibly stressful time in his life, as he felt responsible for all his staff to make sure they could feed their families. He was also the sole provider for his family.

Mark's family and employees stood by his side. They made it through the tough times and came back stronger than ever. His business was having record years.

Things were extremely good. Mark continued to push to help ensure they stayed that way.

He was on vacation in Hawaii and began to experience serious chest pains. When he got home, he went through a series of tests. They found out two things. First, he had a very healthy heart. He did, however, have kidney cancer. They found the kidney cancer by chance and by a miracle.

Mark and I talked about both his chest pains and his kidney cancer. The reason for his chest pains remained undiagnosed. We talked about the possibility of stress. It didn't resonate with Mark because he wasn't feeling stressed. Life was good. His family was great; his business was great. However, Mark had continued to push just as hard when things turned around. His body, like mine, had said, "Enough is enough." Mark needed to start taking care of himself. It resonated with him when we talked about how his chest pain wasn't a physical issue; it was an emotional issue creating a physical problem.

He also felt it was a blessing, because without undergoing the tests he did for his heart, he would never have uncovered the kidney cancer. It turned out, when they operated, that it was an extremely aggressive kind, and they removed his kidney. His doctor told him that if it hadn't been discovered, the cancer would have killed him.

Mark changed his lifestyle both out of necessity, because he only had one kidney, and to make his health a priority. He now takes time away from his business each day to walk. He has changed his diet. He is taking more time for himself, creating some balance at home, and working to reduce his blood pressure. He lost weight and got himself in great shape.

Mark is a very religious guy. He is also one of the most positive people I've ever met. He has had several checkups since his cancer, and he is in great health.

We talk at least once a month to catch up and support each other. One day when we were talking, what he said about his cancer surprised me. And I also agree with him.

He felt his kidney cancer was also caused by stress. Reduction of stress for him was not just about getting rid of his chest pains and lowering his blood pressure; it was to help prevent the return of his cancer as well. I would never have thought that Mark would attribute his cancer to stress.

The interesting thing for both of us is that once we slowed down and took care of ourselves, our bodies and our mental and emotional states, we only experienced more success. Our businesses continued to thrive. Mark has had record year after record year. We more than doubled the revenue of one of my businesses; I sold it, and I now get to focus on coaching and speaking. Not pushing and driving ourselves so hard out of fear of failure and taking care of ourselves only brought greater rewards for us and those in our lives.

I believe we have to take charge and take care of ourselves. We are responsible for being our own best advocates as well as advocates and support for each other. I do believe in paying it forward and that we can all help each other. We can share what we learn. To know that my conversation with Chris helped him and his wife have the children they so desperately wanted feels indescribable to me.

It is why I've written this book. I can only share so much one on one. If what I share here helps create more awareness and helps people solve physical issues caused by stress, then my journey and this book will have served its purpose.

CHAPTER 13

My Personal Top 15 Lessons Learned

During the time I was journaling, I decided one day to put together a list of what I've learned. I did so in order to have a list I could go back to in order to remind myself and reinforce what I'd learned.

Below are some of the key lessons I've shared throughout the book. I wanted to put them in one place so, if you wanted to, you could remember and also share more easily with others. They are in no particular order.

What I've Learned

1. I need to take care of myself along with others. These goals are not mutually exclusive.
2. I've gained perspective. I've learned much more about what is important and what is not.

3. I need to allow my friends and family to take care of me, just as I want to take care of them. I need to let them in, let them help me, and realize they want to help. By not doing so, I am not honoring them and our relationship.
4. I want to give back. I want to use these experiences to help others, should they want my help. It's not about what I've done or accomplished; it's about sharing what I've learned. It's about helping others look within themselves so they can grow as well.
5. I will be grateful every day for my health and all that I have in my life. I will never take this life and all I have for granted.
6. I recognize this is a journey. I will continue on a path of personal growth for my own benefit as well as that of others.
7. I have learned to see the positive in very challenging situations. I know others have it worse—in many cases, much worse.
8. I believe more and more that coincidences occur infrequently and much of what happens does so for a reason. It's up to us to figure out the meaning.
9. I want to continue to grow spiritually and holistically. For me, I want to do so through Qi Gong to provide a combination of meditation and healing in a way that works for my personality and style. I also want to make sure I continue to take care of myself through massage, acupuncture, and other bodywork.

10. The mind is so powerful and can create and manifest so much of what happens in our lives. It's up to each of us to manifest what we want.
11. I am learning how to stress less and worry less and be more at peace. This is going to be an ongoing challenge, as it hasn't been my nature. The things I discussed above about meditation and Qi Gong will help. I need to continue to work in this area and make sure I keep things in perspective. I need to work on not straining my body when there is no need for it.
12. I need to learn to be in the moment—to stop always thinking about the past and the future, to enjoy each moment, to stop and smell the roses, to pay attention to the beauty around me.
13. I will not set limits on myself. At the same time, I will respect what I and my body are capable of. I will be open to whatever success and incredible things might happen to me. I will work to make things better while at the same time having gratitude for all I have and am.
14. My health is my priority. I still push it to the background far too often. I need to be grateful and thankful every day for my health and do what I need to do to take care of myself and my body.
15. I have learned to set boundaries. I am learning to take care of myself and ask for what I need. I am doing so not at the expense of others but while respecting others and their needs as well.

I periodically reread this list to remind myself of my personal commitments and what I've learned. If you have a personal story you would like to share that you feel could help others, I would appreciate you sending it to me at mlevin@csiconsultinginc.com.

Now that I've completed this book, I'm very glad I wrote it. For each of you who read it, I hope you get something out of it that helps you, others in your life, or both.

www.ingramcontent.com/pod-product-compliance
Lightning Source LLC
Chambersburg PA
CBHW070103120526
44588CB00034B/2149